Daughters
of the Moon

Sisters
of the
Sun

Daughters of the Moon Sisters of the Sun

Young Women & Mentors on the Transition to Womanhood

K. Wind Hughes and Linda Wolf
Photography by Linda Wolf

NEW SOCIETY PUBLISHERS

Cataloguing in Publication Data:
A catalog record for this publication is available from the Library of Congress and the National Library of Canada.

Cover design by Miriam MacPhail from a photograph by Gay Marshall.
Book design by Miriam MacPhail.

Printed in Canada on acid-free, partially recycled (20 percent post-consumer) paper using soy-based inks by Best Book Manufacturers.

Inquiries regarding requests to reprint all or part of *Daughters of the Moon, Sisters of the Sun* should be addressed to New Society Publishers at the address below.

Paperback ISBN: 0-86571-377-4
Hardback ISBN: 0-86571-376-6

To order directly from the publishers, please add $3.00 to the price of the first copy, and $1.00 for each additional copy (plus GST in Canada). Send check or money order to:

New Society Publishers,
P.O. Box 189, Gabriola Island, BC V0R 1X0, Canada.

New Society Publishers aims to publish books for fundamental social change through nonviolent action. We focus especially on sustainable living, progressive leadership, and educational and parenting resources. Our full list of books can be browsed on the world wide web at:
http://www.swifty.com/nsp/

NEW SOCIETY PUBLISHERS
Gabriola Island, BC, Canada and New Haven, CT, U.S.A.

I dedicate this book to the unfoldment of spirit:
Gate, gate, paragate, parasamgate, bodhi svaha.
— Wind

To my beloveds: Tom, Heather and Genevieve.
— Linda

And in loving memory of
April Principio-LaSalata, Danaan Parry,
and Amy Anderson.

Contents

Daughters of the Moon, Sisters of the Sun

FOUR: FINDING OUR POWER   137

FIVE: GENDERTALKS   203

Acknowledgments

We are so grateful for all of the people in our lives who have shared themselves with us and are a part of our spirits. Even if we do not mention your name, you are truly a part of this book and we are thankful for your contribution to our lives.

For my life partner Christopher: When Wind and Ocean meet, God becomes manifest. To my Mom, who convinced me I can do anything: Thank you for all of your faith, love, and friendship. To my children, Kimberly and Justin, and 'my adopted daughter,' Maureen: There are no words to describe my love for you. Thanks for hanging in there through everything. For my stepchildren, Cara and Airell: Thank you for your willingness to let me in. You are added love and joy! For my sister Valerie: Your e-mails kept me going with love, encouragement, and humor. To Linda: The laughter and the tears are etched in my inner canvas. Thanks for being who you are and loving me no matter what. I couldn't have done this without you! For Cuz Joe: Thanks for the tips. For the women friends in my life - Laurie G., Penny V., Jerilyn B., Gloria C., Charlene C., Lynne M.: You are always in my heart. For my soul sister Shelly: What a long strange trip it's been! To my ritual circle sisters: Without you, this book would not have been written. For my soul brother Billy: We don't need no stinkin' badges! To my buddy Russell, "and I won't back down!" Chuck: If your thought dreams could be seen...Thanks old friend. To the Grandmothers and Grandfathers: I am listening.

— Wind

To my beloved Tom - husband, best friend, brother, lover, soul mate: Thank you for loving and accepting me completely and supporting me to find love in myself. To our precious daughters, Heather and Genevieve: Thank you for your tenderness, goodness, true love, and compassion. You are the greatest blessings of my life and the inspiration for everything I do. Thank you Mom, for always being there for me. As I listened to all the great women and girls speak their wisdom, I realized everything they said I had already heard from you. Thank you Dad and Diana, for keeping your hearts open as I grow. Thank you Grandma Carrie, for all the late-night soul retrievals. I learned what it felt like to be totally real when I was with you. Thank you Lindsay, for holding me at the depths of my pain and continuing always to be my friend. Oyboyfyboyhidho. Thanks to my soul sisters, Mimi, Andee, Lita, Francie, Jean, Leah, Sara, Libba, Kimberle, Kenzie, Deanna, and sweet Colleen: You are my ocean. Love to the Smeeths, Franklins, Laffertys, Harrisons, and Renches, and special thanks to Einar Kloven for giving me an incredible room of my own. Deep gratitude to Fritjof, for loving friendship; Jackson, for inspiration; Steve, for believing in me; and Jay, for opening up my eyes. And finally sister Wind - you are a constant blessing in my life. These have been three of the greatest years of my life.

— Linda

This book is a deeply collaborative effort. We are especially grateful to the focus group members: You have truly been inspirations and we are so encouraged and hopeful that our future is in your hands. Though your story may not be in print, it is imprinted in our hearts and souls.

Lindsay Allen, Natalie Covert, Eeah, Emily Erickson, Erin Eychaner, Megan Farley, Valerie Fox, Hoku Gearheard, Christin Gordanier, Erika Guidrey, McKayla Hauschulz, Bobbi Hervin, Morgan Hohn, Annie Huntley, Nykky Kesti, Lindsay Killette, Amber Lamareau, Sadie Lien, Sarah Lindsley, Meaghan Mounger, Lorilee Morsette, Shreve Neff, McKenzie Nielsen, Jessi & Janaka Old Coyote, Ara Jane Olufson, Megan Owens, Lisa Richmond, Airyka Rockefeller, Carla Schmidt, Tia Sharpe, Ariel Stallings, Deanna Teasley, and Talina Wood.

Charlie Beil, Shawn Cooper, Patrick Crogan, Morgan Darrah, Josh Davies, Shane Gray, Hookon Haakenson, Jeb Haber, Justin Hoffman, Jacob Lang, Damon McCutcheon, Alex Pinchot, Dennis Plantz, Robin Williams, Rory O'Sullivan, Kyle Schei, Chris Stockton, Seth Topper, and Anthony Yaeger. Eternal thanks to Christopher Love: You are one conscious brother! Also, great thanks to Michael Donnais, David Kotz, Tom Smeeth, and Kris Van Gieson for assisting Christoper from time to time.

Great appreciation to Christopher and Judith Plant and everyone at New Society Publishers including Shannon, Will, Lisa, Gail, and Audrey McClellan for final editing: We knew immediately you were the right midwives for our creative process. You are gifts to the evolution of our planet. Special thanks to Robert and Diane Gilman, without whom this would not have happened. And to Barbara Moulton, our agent and friend, thank you so much for all you did.

Profound gratitude to our advisors and mentors over the years, in particular Maya

Daughters of the Moon, Sisters of the Sun

Angelou, Riane Eisler, Carol Gilligan, Jean Kilbourne, Gabrielle Roth, Barbara Walker, Lindsay Wagner, and Marion Woodman. Bella Abzug, Michelle Akers, Angeles Arrien, Hallie Iglehart Austin, Byllye Avery, Judith Baca, Robert Bly, Deb Boyer, Jerilyn Brusseau, Fritjof Capra, Angela Davis, Vicki Edmonds, Matthew Fox, Arvonne Frazer, Laurie Greig, Esther 'Little Dove' John, Mona Lake Jones, Shiriki Kumanyika, Piper Laurie, Wilma Mankiller, Janet McCloud, Michael Meade, Kate Nobel, Vicki Noble, Amy Ray, Anisa Romero, Emily Saliers, Starhawk, Laura Vescey, and Joan White: Your work and your words of wisdom and support have been inspirational for us.

Sincere thanks to the board of directors of the Daughters/Sisters Foundation for your invaluable contributions: Falilat Olabisi Amoo, Kate Carruthers, Morgan Hohn, Suzanne Lindsley, Christopher Love, Jessi Old Coyote, Elizabeth Pinchot, and Tom Smeeth.

To all our wonderful friends and community on Bainbridge Island, who have given of their time as editors, guest speakers, media techs, transcribers, fundraisers, donators, and in ways too numerous to mention: We could not have accomplished this without your belief in us and in our work. In particular: Joel Brokaw, Jane Brooks, Lisa Down, Jane Engel, Tom Fallat, Rebecca Granato, Emily Grice, Patrick and Gay Marshall, Althea Poulson, Cliff McCrath, Althea Poulson, Jeff Spears, Kristy Tonti, Sara Van Gelder, the staff at *Yes! A Journal of Postive Futures*, and Context Institute. Thanks also to Hazel Cameron and the Juvenile Rehabilitation Administration, Diane Eggleston, Ramee Fair, Kay Jensen, Ana Kincaid, Laura King, Vicki Robin, Lisa Thomas, Barb Zimmer, Rebecca Williamson and everyone at Panda Lab in Seattle.

Thanks to the countless individuals and corporations who have donated to the Daughter/Sisters Project. We could not have done this book without your generous support of our focus groups, workshops, and conferences. Particular thanks to Eve Alvord, the DiSantis family, Anne Gould Hauberg, Laura Ingham, Janet Wright Ketcham, Alida Latham, Carol Luxford, Robin Marks, Elizabeth and Gifford Pinchot, Paula Rees, Francie Rehwald, the Soman-Faulkners, Margaret Taylor, Lindsay Wagner, Virginia Wyman, Adobe Systems, Bainbridge Island School District, Electravoice, Progressive Networks, Sony Inc., and Sound Sound.

And special thanks to the car-pool kids and families whose patience has been incredible: Ruthy & Jenny for the beautiful cover shot; the Linnes and the Langs; and especially John Koriath, Andrea Moncada, Chuck Estin and the kids at Nova Project School who designed our web site and keeps it up and running. You're the best!

Gabrielle Roth

The Moon is the symbol of the female, and we are all daughters of women.

The Sun is the symbol of the male — our brothers, fathers, lovers, and friends.

Daughters of the Moon, Sisters of the Sun
embraces the realization that it takes all of humankind
to come together in understanding and compassion
if we are to create peace, heal the Earth, and celebrate the dance of life.

Introduction

*T*his book is a labor of love and a record of courage, strength, and self-discovery. At its heart are the voices of nearly fifty girls from diverse backgrounds, between the ages of thirteen and twenty-three, who participated in our focus group from 1994 to 1997 and who let us in to share their stories and struggles.

We formed the Girls Focus Group in May 1994 in order to understand what girls today are going through and what they would want addressed in a book for them. Our goal was to create a safe place to be real, not to judge whether someone or something said was right or wrong, acceptable or unacceptable. Part of how we developed safety for the girls to take the risk of sharing their voices was by honestly, and candidly, sharing our own. We also agreed that we would never discuss issues raised in the focus group outside our circle; the girls whose stories appear in this book chose to share them with you.

We came to this work for the sake of ourselves, our children, and the generations to come. As women, we have worked to heal and grow from events in our lives and our own teenage years, and we have learned to cele-

brate and honor the feminine energy in ourselves and in all of life. Our intention has been to empower young women, to help them honor who they are and see life as a continuum - like the cycles and rhythms in nature. We believe that there was a time in our history when elders welcomed young women into the community by initiating them nonviolently into the ways of life and celebrating their transition into womanhood. As we met with the girls in our group and workshops and shared with the mentors, we were aware of how much this vision inspired our work. We are that circle of elders, sitting around the fire with the next generation, sharing our stories, our mistakes, and our wisdom, and listening to each other's experiences, ideals, and plans for the future of our world.

One of the biggest obstacles in the beginning was when we asked the girls what they felt. They would answer, "I don't know." We responded, "Girls, you do know and we'll sit here as long as you need to, until you are quiet enough to listen deeply within yourself and it will come." With that permission to go deeper, beyond self-doubt, the floodgates opened and we discussed everything: sex, love, drugs, parents, homosexuality, boys, body image, dreams, rape, molestation, con-

flict, race, the history of women, religion, music, spirituality, politics, economics. What became immediately clear was how great a need girls had to talk honestly with each other and with older women. Rarely did girls miss sessions; even when one girl ran away from home and quit school, she continued to come to focus group. We anticipated meeting weekly for ten weeks. We ended up meeting for two years. We had no maps to follow. We simply allowed the process to lead us.

The Girls Focus Group had been meeting for about a year when we introduced young men into the process and held the first GenderTalks to help us explore cooperative partnerships and relationships with young men. It was clear after that meeting that the guys needed to develop a deeper connection to their emotions and to acquire more effective communication skills. Therefore, we created a Boys Focus Group, which Christopher Love facilitated for a year, before we held the next GenderTalks.

When we resumed the GenderTalks, it was obvious that the guys had reached some very deep levels, which you will read about in Section Five, in Christopher's story, "Navigating the High Seas of Relationship." They talked about the pain and the sadness they feel because some women fear and mistrust them. They described the shame they feel being associated with the violence, brutality, and injustice that many men have inflicted on

Daughters of the Moon, Sisters of the Sun

women historically and still do today.

Beginning in 1996, we met privately with specific girls - many from the focus group, as well as others who had participated as guests to the project or in the workshops we offered. Our intention was to capture their stories and to show the healing and growth processes they had gone through over the years we knew them. We sent project and book descriptions to some of the most exceptional women in the United States and invited them to be mentors to the girls. Some of them came to the focus group and met with us, while others were interviewed by girls in person or by phone. Many of those interviews appear in this book.

Another contribution to this book came in 1995 when our nonprofit organization, the Daughters/Sisters Foundation, with the help of hundreds of donations, sent Morgan Hohn to represent us at the forum for nongovernmental organizations held in conjunction with the United Nations World Conference on Women in Beijing. Morgan, one of the focus group girls, used what she had learned in the group to facilitate an international Girls Focus Group. She returned with news of the women of the world, which you will read about in her powerful essay, "What the Women of the World Want," in Section Four.

This book is about reclaiming our voices, speaking our truth, and being willing to take the consequences. We hope it will inspire you to take the risk to be yourselves. We hope you find friends in this book. All the girls in this book, as well as the two of us, want to hear from you. You can write to us at: The Daughters/Sisters Project, Box 4586, RollingBay, Washington, 98061; our e-mail address is: daughtersi@aol.com. We also invite you to visit our web site at: http://www.daughters-sisters.org. We encourage you to form your own focus groups and GenderTalks groups and to find other wise women and men to share with.

The girls in the focus group were committed to the process of finding out who they are, and what they felt. They also wanted to share their lives for all the world to hear in the hope that their stories, and the interviews they did, might help other young women find their way a little easier and help them know they are not alone, and that they don't have to be the same, or make the same choices. Their stories are not snapshots of problems without solutions, nor are they simple solutions to lives neatly worked out. They are examples of lives in the process of an ongoing reaching out for truth and connection. They are mirrors in which we hope others will see themselves, windows through which others can view the process of self-searching and healing. We ask you to hold these offerings with an open heart.

ONE

THE EMERGING SELF

~

Heather Wolf-Smeeth

My name is Heather. I'm thirteen, in seventh grade at Hyla Middle School, which is an alternative private school. I have two supportive parents and a little sister and a few really good friends.

Daughters of the Moon, Sisters of the Sun

When I was younger I used to play fantasy games - dress up, orphans, and stuff like that - and I used to think, "Oh, if only I was thirteen...." I thought it was so big. Then when I was approaching it I started thinking, "Wait a minute, I want to go back to being five or eight!" I felt like suddenly we were having so many more responsibilities, more homework, so much more to do, and I couldn't be so free anymore. I remember, I think I was nine or ten, and my friend and I were playing soccer and it was very hot and my mom was like, "Take your shirts off," and we were just like, "No way," and then we ended up doing it and I realized that was the last time I was going to be able to do that in a public place. It was sort of sad to think I was uncomfortable and it wasn't going to be the same anymore. On my thirteenth birthday, I went to school and I was in tears all day. It was a little about everything, but I'm sure some of it was because I really didn't want to grow up. I'm not sure if I've accepted it now or what. I ended up not even having a birthday party, which confuses me because for years my mom would say, "When you turn thirteen, we can have something special for you," but when the time came I didn't want to make it such a big deal and have everyone think, "Oh, Heather's thirteen now, which means she's a teenager, she's going to rebel, she's going to want her privacy." All these things I would be expected to be or do.

Right now, I think a lot of girls my age are going through anticipating all the regular body type stuff to start changing - like boobs and periods and having boyfriends. I see a lot of girls my age starting to dress like the women on MTV, totally into showing off their bodies, wearing tight short shorts, tight tank tops, high heel shoes, and red lipstick. I hear girls say behind their backs, "Oh my God, she's sort of a slut." I think part of them is jealous because boys give them attention. It's sort of expected that boys give the girls who are flaunting attention. Sometimes I feel like I *should* flirt the way everybody else does. Like at camp, I went to this party and the girls got in their bikinis and leaned over just to sort of show off what they've got. I think some of them were doing it consciously and I thought, "That can't be the only way to flirt. Why do I have to flirt with my body?" I flirt, but I just don't do it so blatantly. I've always liked guys, since first grade, but I guess I think those girls are jumping into it too fast. I don't even know if they really like the guys or if it's just that they're seeing other people do it like that.

In school, I see a lot of people acting cool, not being able to let themselves enjoy life fully anymore or show themselves for who they are. The truth is, we're all trying to fit in. There are the popular kids, the ones who have followers and always get people saying, "Sit next to me." Then there are the bookie-types who won't loosen up and let go - they're considered kind of dorky and get made fun of. There's always people who get left out or are teased. It's usually the ones who have been hurt the most who hurt others the most. In general, girls, me included, are afraid that no one will stand beside them. They're afraid to be real, to say how they feel. Some act like they don't care. But they do. They're afraid people will talk behind their backs, that they'll be judged, and it's true - they will be. I see everyone doing it. Not just teenage girls or teenagers but adults as well. Even when you try to stand up to it and tell people to stop, it only ends up making things worse. I even have to think twice about saying all I'm saying

right now. I have to be aware of what the repercussions might be because people will judge me. Me and every single person in this book.

Since I've been little, I've always stood up for people. I haven't really been worried about my place in the whole social thing. I think people think of me as someone who is independent and assertive and herself. Being funny and laughing has been an easy way for me to fit in and still be out there and different, but I feel I'm pretty accepted. I hope when I'm not that it wouldn't be that big of a deal for me, that I'd just keep being myself. I know if I started acting like someone else just to be cool, I wouldn't feel good about myself and I would hate myself more than if I was myself and everybody thought I was out of it. Often, though, I feel like there's no one I can relate to. I feel so many people my age are so shallow.

These days I feel like friendship is a tricky thing. Very quickly you learn who you can't tell secrets to and who you have to be wary of. Yet actually, I think it's a good thing. I don't think you need to tell everyone everything. What really confuses me, though, is that

Daughters of the Moon, Sisters of the Sun

sometimes I'll talk with a person one night and I'll think they understand what I'm saying, but the next day it won't seem that way anymore. Same thing when you think a guy likes you and you get your hopes up, only to find out that it was just for that one night and it wasn't anything at all - just false hopes.

Personally, I don't like being this age. It's the same pattern every day. Get up, go to school, come home, do homework, go to bed, and do the same thing all over again the next day. A lot of what goes on at this age is, "Does he like me, doesn't he like me? Am I fitting in? What are they saying about me behind my back? What are they thinking about me? Oh, if I say this, they'll all think I'm so stupid. Oh my gosh, I just made the biggest fool of myself by saying that." But it's important to keep all the stuff that's going on in my life right now in perspective because if I get wrapped up in every little thing, I won't be able to see the bigger picture. A month or a year from now, I'm not even going to remember what was so important, what people said or wore or who's fighting with who.

I'm not in a rush to do any of the stuff kids my age are starting to get into - like

drugs or alcohol. I think there's only one or two people getting into drugs, but most of us still feel we're pretty young for that. I'm sure I will try it someday and I think I'll get something out of it too, but I'm not in any rush and that's fine. Besides, there are so many people in this world, I can cultivate people around me that don't always need to be high. For me, enjoying life is a natural high. I loved that movie, *Dead Poets Society*, and how it's about sucking the marrow out of life. It inspired me, made me realize there's so much more to life.

I don't like to think about all the bad stuff going on in the world - the ozone hole, the pollution and population crisis. It makes me depressed. I consider myself a conscious person. I'm aware and I care about the world, but I don't feel like I can change much of it. I try to help other people become more aware, but I end up getting mad and frustrated - both about all the world problems and about the people who don't listen or understand. Often teachers will ask us to think about what we'll be doing in twenty, thirty years, but I don't

think most kids want to think about what might happen if we don't clean up the environment, get a hold on the economy, and stop polluting everything.

I'm making it sound like everything's all negative. It really isn't. It's only one side of the story. The other is just about having fun, being friends, and laughing a lot. Even regular, stable school is good. Being able to hang out at break, having sunny days, and being able to go sit on the grass and eat outside - just hanging out with friends. It feels refreshing not to have to always be so serious or make everything so deep.

I try very hard to live by the saying "To thine own self be true" and to live life for myself because, ultimately, no one else is going to get anything out of it but me. I work hard to let people be who they are, knowing that any amount of judging them won't change them. There are many things I can say I need in life, but when it comes down to it, the only thing that will make me happy when I'm having a bad day is knowing I'm wanted, that people would rather have me in this world than not. Because there are those times when you forget how it feels to be alive, you forget you would rather be in this world than not be in it. For me the most important thing is to laugh. I need to laugh my whole entire life. Laugh so much people think I'm crazy and then get them laughing with me.

Carol Gilligan talks with the Girls Focus Group

Carol Gilligan is a professor in the Human Development and Psychology Program at the Graduate School of Education, Harvard University, and author of groundbreaking feminist works including In a Different Voice *and* Meeting At The Crossroads *(with Lyn Mikel Brown).*

Carol: After writing *In a Different Voice,* which was about bringing women's voices into what was called the 'human conversation,' I realized that the word 'girl' was missing from the descriptions of women's psychology and that when people talked about child or adolescent psychology, they were often speaking about research or theories that were based on studies of boys only. It was amazing to realize how often girls had been left out of psychology research and how much of psychology was written without anyone listening to girls. So with a group of women who were graduate students at Harvard where I teach, I began what turned into a real voyage of discovery.

We found we had forgotten a girl's world that we once had known. Listening to girls, we heard a vitality and strength that we found both familiar and surprising; we were struck by the clarity of girls' perception and their courage in speaking their minds and hearts. What we learned was how much girls know and how astutely girls watch and pick up on what's going on around them, how intently they listen in to the human world. Our research into women's psychological history started with adolescent girls; then we went back further into childhood and worked with girls who were between six and eleven years old, and followed them as they grew into teenagers. When I first began writing about this work in the late 1980s, I was amazed by the response; everyone seemed to know what I was talking about, although no one had been talking about girls.

In 1989, my colleague Annie Rogers and I started a project called 'Strengthening Healthy Resistance and Courage in Girls,' and with Normi Noel - a voice and theater teacher - we formed theater, writing, and outing clubs with girls, where we met weekly, sort of the way you are doing here in the focus group. We saw girls fighting to stay in relationship - not to mute their voices or lose connection with themselves or other people or the world they lived in. We saw that as the girls approached adolescence, they were under increasing pressure from outside, and also from within themselves, to not know what they knew or not feel what they felt or not say what they meant or not care about what they really cared about. Girls were in danger of drowning or disappearing because surfacing in relationships or speaking for themselves often seemed to put them and their relationships at risk. It was confusing, because girls' strengths were putting girls at risk.

Many people now have written about girls losing their self-esteem when they reach adolescence, but often they don't say why girls are losing their sense of self-worth or what is at stake when teenage girls continue to speak with clarity and courage. It isn't as though girls develop a leak at adolescence and self-esteem just runs out of them. Over and over again in our research, we heard girls describe a real problem which we could observe with them: if they said what they were feeling and thinking, they were in danger of losing their relationships; but if they didn't speak their minds and their hearts, they would be out of relationship and no one would know what was happening for them. The truth of this observation was striking to us, and we watched girls make brilliant but sometimes very costly moves to try and find ways of staying in connection with others without losing touch with their own inner world. The emphasis on loss of self-esteem diverted attention from the nature of the struggle and what was at stake, not only for girls but for everyone. Girls were facing head-on a psychological disconnection which is often confused in this society with independence and freedom.

As I hung out with girls, sat in on their classes, and went to their homes, I was struck by how often I heard people tell girls not to speak or not to speak in public, or watched people communicate to girls in one way or another that others don't want to hear what they think and feel, won't want to be with them, or won't appreciate what they have to say. Girls began to modulate their voices when they realized that when they spoke freely

their voices sounded too loud or too assertive or too angry or too out of line. Repeatedly, girls would name the dilemma: if they continued to speak their minds and their hearts, people would not want to be with them, but if they didn't say what they were feeling and

thinking, nobody would be connected with them. Either way they would be all alone. As girls confronted and named this problem of relationship - how to maintain connection - they looked to women, asking women, "Where are you in this?" And also observing what women were doing and what women are willing to say to girls about what they are doing and about what they know.

We discovered how challenging it is for

women to be with girls at this point in girls' development, and to stay in honest relationship with them, because it means coming into a more honest relationship with ourselves and asking ourselves what we are doing and what we know and often don't know, or why we act as if we didn't know. Through our writing and theater group with girls and one another, our voices were changing and we were becoming more direct and more courageous with one another and ourselves. Learning from girls, we began to speak more from experience, talking with girls about what we knew about ways of being in the world and being with others while staying in touch with ourselves. It became essential in this work for us, the three women, to work through our own stuff as well, because being with girls brought up a lot and affected our relationships with one another and with other people in our lives. We saw that there is a lot of pressure on girls and women to turn away from one another. There is a kind of complicity in this turning away: "If you don't look at me or say what you see or hear me doing, I won't look at you or speak about what I see or hear you doing." And we began to ask the obvious question: Why don't

girls and women turn towards each other at this point, instead of turning away? Then we could struggle together with the real dilemma for all of us: What would it mean to keep our voices strong in the world and toreally care about being in relationship with people?

Linda: What kind of healthy resistance are you talking about? And what are these brilliant but costly struggles that are dangerous?

Carol: You probably know from your own experience that up until girls become teenagers, it's usually boys who are in trouble - whereas girls show surprising psychological strength and resilience during childhood. Like in school, who gets sent to counselors? The boys. So what's going on with the girls?

Annie: While boys are being bad, girls are being eager to please.

Carol: You could say "eager to please," but you can also say figuring it out, psyching it out, figuring out how to do school. A lot of what girls do that is very strong and savvy gets called names that sound bad. I think there's a lot of honesty among girls about what's going on. Healthy resistance is about staying in touch with your mind and your heart. It takes courage. There's a wonderful

Old English definition of the word 'courage': "To speak your mind by telling all your heart." I think girls do that and often they're able to differentiate between real relationships and false relationships, only speaking, opening up in relationships that are true. Staying in touch is knowing what you know and resisting dissociation.

Annie: I censor myself a lot. I say to myself, "Don't say that" or "They don't agree with you, so just keep your mouth shut." I know it's no good to do that but it's easier.

McKenzie: I think it has a lot to do with learning the system. You say something wrong once and someone gets mad and you start to develop an inner censor. By the time you're a senior, you have all these inner censors and so almost nothing you think can get through the filters. You have this surface personality that talks for you, that is pleasing to everyone and is different in every situation.

Carol: That's exactly what I would say is a brilliant but costly solution because that censor that senses every situation and figures out how to deal with it is almost like a face in front of your face. It speaks for you and gets harder and harder. If you think you are going to say something wrong or stupid or whatever, then it's a good thing not to speak at all because you don't want to have what really matters to you invalidated by other people. But the cost of not speaking is great. It's a brilliant way to protect yourself but it's very costly. So I think we should congratulate the psyche on her great wisdom and at the same time wonder if there are better ways to deal with it.

Meaghan: I used to have to censor so much of the time that I couldn't tell which was which. Now I feel I have people I can be more up-front with. But I still do it. I can feel when I go into it and I do it consciously because I don't like certain people to know who I am, because it's unsafe.

Erin: A lot of times manipulation sounds cold and hard, but when you're dealing with people you work with, it's really necessary.

Carol: I don't hear this as a bad thing. I know it's a big negative thing for women, that women are manipulative. But what does it mean, 'manipulate'? It comes from 'manus,' 'hand.' People who don't understand the human world - a lot of men, a lot of adults who have forgotten - are uncomfortable when people can read it, and then it gets called manipulation. It's a perfect example of taking a common strength among girls and giving it a bad name. You can't be manipulative unless you understand the world. How did you learn that? Going to school, living in your house, you watch and listen and put things together and figure it out. You can use it for good ends and you can use it to hurt people. And it would be crazy to act as if you didn't know. Except, of course, there's a lot of pressure on girls not to know. What we saw in doing our work is that around the time girls become teenagers, they start saying, "I don't know, I don't remember, I don't know." Yet the year before, they knew. So it's like - wait a minute, what happened?

Linda: Do you think the more we do that sort of manipulation, though, the easier it is to lose touch with ourselves and to start forgetting? Is that why you practiced knowing what you know with the girls in your group?

Carol. Yeah - I think it is true.

Linda: So the more we mask ourselves or manipulate truth or rearrange ourselves in order to keep safe, the more distant we become from ourselves, until we finally forget how to be close to ourselves. We become adults who've forgotten and then have to go back and find it.

Carol: It seems to me that the question is, is it possible to be with people and have your feelings? What would it take? And how much, in different ways, in different places, on different days, do each of us feel we have to give up our feelings or our thoughts in order to be with people and then it doesn't work because we're not really *with* people? It strikes me, in a group like this, that's something you can explore with each other.

Daughters of the Moon, Sisters of the Sun

Maiden, Mother, Crone

Wind Hughes

I wish that when I was younger someone had shared with me an understanding of a woman's life cycle. Something more profound than "You must save for retirement;" something that honored the changes I would be going through rather than the social fear of growing old.

We are always changing and transforming ourselves. If we clung to what once was, we would be resisting the natural changes and rhythms of our being. Imagine if trees hung on to their leaves and didn't allow them to drop in the fall. The branches would not be bare in the winter, so the tree would send nutrients to the old leaves when it should be sending all of its energy to the inner tree, preparing for the spring. In the spring, the new leaves would not come through because the old leaves were blocking their way. We have seasons of our lives just like the trees, and it helps to understand how we move through them.

There are many ways to explore the changing stages of a woman's life. One way is to see the cycles reflected in the three stages of the Triple Goddess: the Maiden, the Mother, and the Crone. Many cultures have myths of the Triple Goddess. In Greek mythology we find the story of Hera. She is made up of three aspects: Hebe, the Virgin (Maiden); Hera, the Mother; Theria, the Crone. On February 2, Celtic tradition honors Brigid, whose three aspects are called the Three Blessed Ladies. The French, on May 24, honor the Mother of

Arles, another triple myth. The Moon Goddess is celebrated in Greece on November 16. Her Maiden is Artemis, her Mother is Selene, and her Crone is Hecate. All of these myths speak about the cycles of the feminine, the changing seasons in nature, and the life cycle of birth, death, and rebirth.

Particular tasks are best accomplished at certain stages of the cycle. When the tasks of one stage are achieved, a solid foundation is laid for the following stage. It's like building a house. If the foundation is not solid and well built, eventually the house - no matter how beautiful - will begin to show signs of stress and strain until one day the residents have to jack the house up so they can get underneath to reinforce the foundation. If we have not properly completed the earlier tasks in our lives, we too, at a later date, may have to 'jack up' parts of ourselves so we can get underneath to deeper levels of earlier experiences and make 'repairs.'

Each stage is symbolized by a woman of a particular age and stage of life, an *archetype*. Think of an archetype as an aspect of the human experience that continually occurs, a pattern of behavior that is represented by a symbolic personality. We embody aspects of the Maiden, Mother, and Crone within us always, yet we can see where one archetype may more powerfully influence a particular stage of our life. For the sake of understanding our progression through these stages, I will speak of them as symbols of distinct times of our lives.

The Maiden (developing ego): She is a young woman, pure of heart, full of love and curiosity, experimenting with life, trying new things, and having new experiences. She carries the seeds of all potential: anything is possible and all possibilities are within her. She does not limit herself by the needs or beliefs of others. She is in love with the mystery of life. She is whole unto herself and finds complete meaning within herself. Sometimes you may find the Maiden referred to as the Virgin. This does not refer to a girl who has not yet had sex but to one who is whole without other. She is complete by herself.

The dark aspects of the Maiden: She can get lost in her own world, dangerously taking risks, becoming self-destructive, holding a deaf ear to the inner voice of her own wise Crone and to the wisdom of others. She may

be the dutiful daughter, her self-worth linked to pleasing others in order to receive their approval. She has not developed a strong sense of self and may 'lose herself' when she enters the next stage.

The Maiden's job: The Maiden must find herself and her voice. She must come to know her own thoughts, ideas, values, and purpose, and to dream and generate vision for her life. It can be difficult when she doesn't have the encouragement she needs to explore and believe in herself, especially when other people's opinions of her take on more power than her own journey of self-discovery.

The Mother (actualizing ego): The Mother births creation and devotes herself to 'other,' to people and things outside of herself. Often the archetype of the Mother makes you think of a woman giving birth to or devoting herself to a child, but here we are speaking of all of the possibilities of creation. This could be producing a work of art, acquiring knowledge, pursuing a profession - some process that allows the birthing of the creative energy within us. She is a selfless soul whose devotion and love are unconditional. She must choose a focus, a path of some kind, and establish her responsibility and commitment to it. In her choosing lies the creative responsibility for her life. She is taking the visions of the Maiden and manifesting the dreams of *her* choice. The strong self she developed as a Maiden now learns to be humbled in service as she develops selflessness and unconditional giving. It will be a *choice* to act selflessly, not a duty.

The dark aspects of the Mother: We depend on the Mother to nurture us and protect us and so she has the power to abuse and abandon us. She can control, criticize, and reject the young Maiden within us. If she does not have a strong Maiden inside, she may lose herself in the 'other' and dissolve away, taking care of other while *denying* herself, becoming a martyr.

The Mother's job: The Mother actualizes the dreams of the Maiden by allowing and encouraging them to be made manifest in the world. This is a stage where she learns to put someone or something before herself, her ego. If she has a healthy Maiden and Mother inside, she won't lose herself in this process and she can discover a deeper aspect of being. For some, a spiritual awareness is discovered as

the ego is tempered and humbled by love, service, and creation. She begins to find the wisdom of the Crone.

The Crone (surrendering ego): This is a very wise woman. No longer focused on others, she has turned her reflections inward, as the Maiden did. She is not detached from the world, just not involved in the ways she was before. She seeks more solitude. Others seek her out for guidance and she welcomes them. She has a wide perspective gained from years of experience. She has 'been there - done that." She can be completely honest because she has nothing to lose. She holds the wisdom, teaches, and shares stories with those who will listen.

The dark aspects of the Crone: She can be bitter if she did not complete the tasks of the previous stages of life, making it difficult for her to let go of her youth, dreams, people, and life in the body. She may isolate herself and may blame others for her misfortunes. Her rage can be fiery, her sadness and pain deep.

The Crone's job: She is fulfilled by a life well lived, dreams and visions actualized. Her children, if any, are grown. Her responsibility is to share the knowledge that she has acquired, and she welcomes the invitation to share it. She returns the seed of vision back to the Maiden. Within her is a lively Maiden and a creative Mother. Our culture tends to devalue our elders, retiring them from work and often from the family and life in general. We lose so much of ourselves, within and without, when we lose connection with the wisdom of the Crone.

We all have within us the good aspects as well as the dark aspects of these archetypes. If we find Maidens, Mothers, and Crones who can serve as role models, we can learn how they are negotiating the cycles of their lives. Life is a thread of single moments woven together, side by side, creating one continuous experience, each moment separate but connected to the whole.

Talina Wood

My name is Talina. I'm fourteen years old. My father died before I was born, so for most of my life I've lived with my mother and my brother from her second marriage.

I don't believe in a male God. I feel closer to the earth than the sky. I had lots of experience with the Christian God in my childhood because we moved around from church to church, testing them out. By sixth grade I felt the need to belong to one church, so we settled on the Alliance Church. I wanted to know more about God. I wanted to know him. It seemed like all these people knew him so personally.

I tried several times to read the Bible, but it was boring and seemed wrong to me. It made God sound like someone remote, stand-offish, distant, and cold. He cared about humanity as a whole, but it didn't seem that he cared about individuals. As long as humanity was fine, it was okay if a few people were sacrificed. Eventually I stopped going to church, but I still had a longing to know God.

Around this time I started middle school, where I met Lily. She was into the Goddess. Lily was so strong and powerful; she believed in herbs and rituals and doing stuff to bring you closer together with your friends and help your life. I went to the store and found books on candle rituals and stuff, and I thought it was pretty cool. I liked doing them by myself. I was attracted by the mysticism.

When I started doing rituals and looking more into the Goddess, it felt more real and down-to-earth than praying to some nebulous being somewhere in the sky. The Goddess seems like she really cares for people. She seems to connect me more with myself and how I feel. Whenever I go to sleep at night and I get scared, I always think of her and it feels like there's someone there for me, like a warm, secure blanket, and I don't feel alone. It's like she's alive in me and makes me feel spirit more strongly. I never felt that way with Jesus. I love the idea of the priestess healers, how they would help and heal people. In this religion, women are not just here to bear children and carry sin around the world. We have connection.

At graduation for the eighth graders in my school, four of us - Christi, Heather, Lily, and I - went down to the field below our school and had a little ritual to bind us together and make us sisters. We all looked in our individual books of rituals and made it up as we went along. We sat down in a circle, burned candles and sage and incense, and made pledges to each other. We also recited stuff from the texts. To finalize it, we ran and skipped around and danced and screamed and laughed and cried - any expression that felt right at the moment. It was meant to bring us all together, to make us better friends and sisters and to make sure that we'll be friends forever.

That night all the eighth graders had a sleep-over in the all-purpose room at school. Lily and I got the girls who wanted to do a ritual together and we sat down behind a curtain and burned sage and incense. We each took turns doing a ritual about a specific thing involving the others. We had some music and one person would dance and another would shield her from hurting herself or bumping into others. And then we did a screaming thing. We'd breathe in and breathe out, breathe in, breathe out, and on the fifth time we'd express our emotions in some way. Most of the time we wanted to scream, but we'd wait for one of us to start and then we'd all follow with her. We did rituals for three hours until everybody told us to stop because they were choking from the incense.

Recently, I watched the film series *The Burning Times* and couldn't believe what it said about the past. All those women burned and drowned and tortured for being so-called witches. They were just doing what we did. Doing healing spells and herbs and incense. It made me want to cry. To think that in the name of Christ they did all those horrible things to women, just because they wanted their God, Jesus Christ, to be on top. They wanted Christianity to be the dominant religion and so they went about finding people that were doing rituals and called them witches and turned the whole view of these women around. Instead of thinking women were good, healers, they turned it all around and called them evil.

Even today, they say women are all evil because of Eve, that she brought on the fall of humankind. And she probably wasn't even real. It seems they're brainwashing people. They took away something that was special to everyone, just so that they could call us all barbarians, just because we believed in something different and wanted to be independent. It was wrong and terrible.

We're not wrong and sinful because we don't believe in the Christian religion. Women are strong. We have minds and thoughts of our own. We're special. If there weren't any women, we wouldn't be here. Every living being is born from the body of a female. But in our culture, it's like we're only ornaments for men, that's all we are, we're like ornaments on a Christmas tree. It's like guys don't see us.

Maybe they're starting to change now a little bit, but very slowly. They still don't see us as, like, equals. They see us more as beneath them. It's particularly evident to me where religion comes in because you never see any women priests, it's always guys. If I had a choice, I wouldn't go to school. I'd apprentice myself to Starhawk.

I don't remember ever feeling celebrated for being a young woman, but now that I'm becoming aware of the old religion I'm seeing ways to celebrate myself. People still think it's weird to say you don't believe in Jesus; that's what makes me afraid to tell anyone about my beliefs or my rituals. I'm afraid I'll be ostracized. So much could go wrong if I did tell. Almost everyone I know goes to a church and I can't imagine they would accept the Goddess. I feel I would be looked down upon, be called a heathen or some bad word. I imagine that people would be suspicious of me.

Here we live in America where we're supposed to have freedom of religion, but what is this 'freedom' people speak about? It sounds more like freedom to be like them. We're told, "Don't be different, don't deviate." In these people's view, the Goddess is Satan. Well, since I don't believe in that religion, I don't believe there is a Satan. Or a hell for that matter.

I realize people cling to religions because they often fear death, but death to me isn't a bad thing. When I think of dying, I imagine that maybe I'll be reincarnated or maybe I'll just go sit with the Goddess, become part of nature again, and help nourish future generations.

I'd like to share all this with my mom. I know she believes in a higher being. I know she prays to God and I think if she had a chance to start over and think about it, she would go with the Goddess, too. But even if she doesn't, it's my choice. I don't want to estrange myself from her or have her think I'm part of a cult or something; I'm not planning to become a healer or a priestess. I want to connect with the feminine aspect of spirit, that's all.

Talina Wood talks with
Starhawk

*S*tarhawk is the author of many books on the ancient religion of the Goddess.
She is a peace activist and one of the foremost voices of ecofeminism.

Talina: What is your definition of witch and how is it different from being a pagan?

Starhawk: A witch is a person who has a commitment to the Wiccan tradition of the Goddess and to being a priestess, priest, teacher, or healer; someone who takes responsibility for the earth and who connects through ritual with the cycles of birth, growth, death, and rebirth. 'Pagan' is a word that literally means 'countryside.' The pagans were the ones who lived in the country and weren't Christianized as fast as the people who lived in the cities. They worshipped the earth and tended to cling to the old ways and the old understandings.

Talina: What gave people such a bad impression of witches and witchcraft, and why do they call it a cult?

Starhawk: I think the impression was deliberately created over several hundred years by certain factions in the church that wanted to reduce the competition [with Christianity], plus there were a lot of complex economic and social reasons why it served them to let loose a witch persecution. Because of that, the word has taken on a bad name. It takes a lot of work to reeducate people about what it really means.

People tend to think that everything that isn't part of the religion they grew up with is a cult, but the definition of a cult has to do with someone being in charge who has the power to tell other people what to believe, how to think, act, and behave in a way that limits their freedom. It's wise to look out for that in any religion or any tradition. As soon as somebody tells you, "You have to think this. You have to believe that," I say, "Look out." Every spiritual tradition uses ritual and meditation. A ritual is anything we do that honors and gives value to the subject we're doing it about. In the Goddess tradition, we believe strongly that each of us has our own connection with the Goddess.

Talina: Are there sets of laws like the Bible in the Goddess tradition?

Starhawk: There is no set of commandments like the Ten Commandments, but there are a couple of basic principles. One is called the Rule of Three, which says that anything you send out magically returns to you three times over. So if you're sending out healing energies and love, you tend to attract that kind of energy to you, but if you are sending out harm or hate or are cursing somebody, then you would attract three times that energy. In a sense it's like the Golden Rule; you can't do to others what you don't want to have happen to you.

Talina: How can a person integrate the Goddess into everyday life?

Starhawk: When you eat dinner, make sure you compost your garbage instead of throwing it in the trash. Be conscious when you use energy or buy things; be careful not to pollute; pick up trash on the ground even though it isn't yours - these are daily ways of honoring the Goddess and taking care of the earth. It's also important and helpful to develop some sort of personal practice, something you do specifically for yourself every day. For me it may be a specific meditation or taking a walk or sitting down on the earth and grounding myself as a way to honor my body and say that it's sacred. Sometimes it might be making an offering. Lately, I leave a bowl of milk out for the fairies every night. What I try to do whenever I can is spend some time in nature, observing, just noticing all the different complexities of the plants and animals and the soil and the way things grow and the patterns.

Talina: Christianity advises against premarital sex. What are your views on teenage sex and gay and lesbian relationships?

Starhawk: Unfortunately in this day and age you have to be very careful about sex and be very responsible to protect yourself. But I think the teenage years are a time when your sexuality is rising and you want to explore and try it out. In an ideal world I would like to see teenagers free to explore and experiment and enjoy their sexuality and do it safely. In the Goddess tradition, sexuality is sacred in all its forms. So if two women love each other, or two men, and they give each other pleasure, that's a way of honoring the Goddess. We don't say that there's only one kind of sexuality that's clean and the rest is dirty; we say that all the different ways that people love each other are sacred. In the poem "The Charge of the Goddess," the Goddess says, "All acts of love and pleasure are my rituals." Today, with the AIDS epidemic threatening so many lives, it is more important than ever to assert the sacredness of the erotic.

Daughters of the Moon, Sisters of the Sun

Marianna Pinchot and Heather Wolf-Smeeth talk with Riane Eisler

Riane Eisler is the author of The Chalice and the Blade, The Partnership Way, and Sacred Pleasure. She is a cultural historian and lecturer and codirector of the Center for Partnership Studies in California. Marianna Pinchot is a friend of Heather's from Hyla Middle School.

Marianna: Do you think the forgetting of the Goddess culture affects the development of the adolescent girl's self-esteem?

Riane: Judy Chicago says, "Women get disappeared in history." The effect of this is to leave us with a history in which we have been essentially deprived of our rightful heritage, a heritage in which women were priestesses - positions women are fighting for today. It is important for us to have a position where we can say what is right and what is wrong. If you are not in the priesthood, you do it from the sidelines, so to speak. So I think [neglect of the Goddess culture] has had a profound disempowering effect on all of us, women and girls, because it doesn't give us the knowledge that we can take leadership positions or have what I call 'moral authority.' It is important to notice how God, the deity, is presented. If there is no feminine aspect of the deity, then you are a second-class person.

Heather: The media is turning into something almost as influential as a religion, isn't it?

Riane: Whoever has control over telling the stories, over presenting the world to us, has enormous power. That used to be, of course, the monopoly of these male-headed, very authoritarian religious institutions. Even though there were some stories that were more partnership-oriented, most presented the world in terms of what I call a 'dominator model.' This danger exists still today, especially with what's happening in the U.S. Congress.

Congress just passed a law that makes it even easier for control over the media to be concentrated in the hands of huge corporations. Many of them aren't even American corporations. One of the most important things we can do is to raise our voices.

Marianna: Do you see a link between the women's rights movement, the environmental movement, and the Goddess religion?

Riane: The exploitation of nature's life-giving and life-supporting activities as men's due, that they're entitled to it, is very much the same mind-set as men dominating women. The idea that women's nurturing work, or what has been relegated until now to women - like taking care of children, taking care of other people's health, taking care of the environment in the house - the idea that that's also been men's due and that women should do it for free with no other options in a male-headed, male-controlled household, is linked.

What is happening now in the United States is dangerous because, on the one hand, the people in Congress are trying to repeal affirmative action, which gave women an option to earn money independently rather than being dependent for their survival. At the

Daughters of the Moon, Sisters of the Sun

same time, these people are trying to defund the public services: the services that care for children, care for people's health, care for the elderly, care for the environment. So there is not only a link between the environmental movement and the women's movement; there's a link in terms of the partnership versus the dominator society. The earlier Goddess-worshipping societies were more partnership-oriented, but it wasn't only because they worshipped the Goddess.

We are in a period of what I call 'dominator regression' right now. Historically, the shift that we're trying to make from a dominator to a partnership way of living started about three hundred years ago when the Industrial Revolution began to go into high gear and there was a lot of destabilization and things started to fall apart. When that happened, there was an opportunity to question things and to look for alternatives. For the past three hundred years we've seen enormous progress. Just think about the gains we've made: access to college, the vote. In the 1960s, want ads were still segregated into "Help Wanted Men" and "Help Wanted Women." The bad jobs, the dead-end jobs, were all listed under "Help Wanted Women." We have to remember we've made a lot of changes already and we need to teach it all year long. There's a grassroots effort for more change, but when there's forward movement, there's resistance.

In the long term, I'm optimistic. In the short term, there's going to be a lot more pain. It's up to you, also, because it's your lives and it's your futures. It won't be easy, but you *can* make a difference.

Bonnie Price

*I am seventeen years old and I was born in New Mexico during the hottest
summer in 180 years. After my eighth birthday we left for eastern Washington
and went to live on a commune in the middle of nowhere, with all the weird
hippies, the Mormons, and all the other people who were trying to get away from
the world.*

Mom and dad got divorced, so we all live on Vashon Island with my mom and we visit dad on weekends. I was raised to have an open mind, and I think my parents had open minds and did an excellent job.

My parents were both Baha'is. I don't know when I knew I was a Baha'i, but it was probably not very early. The premise of the Baha'i faith is that every manifestation of God, and I think there were nine - Zoroaster, Muhammad, Buddha, Jesus - all of them were all just manifestations of the same God, which is the only God, of course. Every culture that I've known has come up with at least an idea of spirituality, even cultures that have never ever come in contact with each other. Why would everybody come up with the same idea if it wasn't true? They're all saying the same thing. Love yourself. Love your neighbor. Love your countrymen. Love your whatever. My spiritual life has mostly gone hand-in-hand with my emotional and physical maturity. I think that's healthy. I've met people who are spiritually mature and emotionally not even there. That scares me, so for me it's gradual.

When I was about thirteen, my mom decided to get her Reiki training and asked me to do it too. Reiki is basically healing by laying on of the hands. Some students in Japan asked their teacher how Jesus healed. To be honorable, he had to go find out. He spent seven years going all around the globe. He came back to Japan, went to the top of some mountain, and God said, "This is how he did it. Here's how you do it. Go teach it." So he did, and it's all over the world.

Everybody in the training gets an attunement. I closed my eyes and the teacher smudged me and guided me into a trance. She asked my spirit guide or guardian angel to come, and mine came. She was actually a person that I had dreamed about a long time ago. She was wearing long, flowing white robes and was more graceful than you could possibly ever conceive. She talked to me for a while and then the teacher said, "Have her give you a gift." She gave me this white lotus.

Later that day, we went back to talk with our spirit guides again. This time, two of them showed up. There was the white lady and there was this woman who I call Oholi Bamah. She was black with real short curly hair. She wore a sarong and was dancing like the power of fire and earth. Both of them were talking to me at the same time, and that's probably the closest I've ever gotten to hearing the voice of God. There were hundreds of layers of harmony going. It was like this huge, booming voice, but it wasn't intrusive at all. I was blown away!

I think that experience opened me to a lot more possibilities of how spirit could be, how anything could be. Like you could touch it if you wanted to, if you needed to. I'm sure you could. I'd always kind of assumed that the physical world and the spiritual world were pretty much separate. After that I knew God, the entity, is in the earth and in everything I touch. It changed my conception of God to more of a universal spirit.

I started my period right after my fourteenth birthday while I was away camping with friends. I was happy because my younger sister was developing really fast and I had been developing really slowly. I thought she was gonna start before me and I was gonna have my birthright taken away. I'm the oldest daughter. I was like, "No, I'm older. I get to be a woman first."

When I got home from camping, I had all these cloth pads that had blood in them and they needed to be soaked out. I wondered what to do with them, so I put them in water in the kitchen sink and left to go to a friend's house for the weekend. I remember thinking, "Oh shit, I left the pads. Mom's gonna be so mad." So she called me up and she was crying and so happy. She said, "Oh I found them."

Then I began to learn about other ceremonies and rituals. We had a ceremony, "The Red Party," to celebrate my beginning to bleed. One day at five o'clock in the morning I wake up and there's people singing outside my window. They were singing, "Go to Bonnie and tell her we love her, and by the light of the moon we will come to her." I thought, "What is going on?" They were holding candles, singing, and their faces were lit from underneath, and I'm thinking, "Where's my mom? Who's there?"

They told me to get up and put on some clothes. I did and they said, "Come with us, woman," and I'm like, "Woman? What's that supposed to mean?" It didn't connect in any way. We got in the van. I asked, "Where are we going?" And the driver said, "I'm not telling." It started to get light. I had no clue where we were. I was totally turned around. We ended up at a friend's house with a huge front yard, enormous trees, and grass.

There was this fire in the field and there were about twenty women all around the fire, all dressed in every kind of red outfit you could possibly imagine. Nan's costume was the best. She had this huge woman sign painted on her face in red lipstick or face paint, and she had tampons braided into her hair. She had this long string that she had pinned on so it looked like a huge tampon string coming out from between her legs. It was hilarious.

Everybody sat around a circle. Mom was all dressed up like a Crone in somebody's sarong. She had this picture of me when I was really little. She asked, "Has anybody seen this girl?" Everybody answered, "No. No." Nobody had seen this girl ... because I wasn't the girl anymore.

I was feeling so frumpy in my horrible old gross purple sweat pants and orange socks and red shoes and my hair! These women were dressed in great red outfits. I thought, "I wish I had known." Then mom brought out this dress, a real simple jumper in a beautiful fabric that she had made. So I took my clothes off and she put the dress on me and everyone sang songs and took pictures. Everybody went around the circle and gave me gifts and told stories. Then I asked them

how many lovers they had had. One person had one. Another person had two. Some people had women lovers and some people had men lovers and some people had women and men lovers. Some said they couldn't count, "It's hundreds!" Mom didn't say. She still hasn't told me. They went around and offered their advice and talked about safe sex and different kinds of contraception. Some people there were Mothers and some of them were Crones and some of them were Maidens. It was pretty outrageous. I was crying.

My first Long Dance must have been just a few weeks later. The reason it's called Long Dance is because it's three or four days long and you dance around the huge bonfire all night long. There's a moon lodge, sweat lodges, and all kinds of projects. People brought tons and tons of herbs and everybody made herbal prayer pouches and threw them into the fire. There's dancing and drumming all night long. I don't think I danced all night, but I danced a lot of the night. I'm a drummer, I play the congas, but I didn't drum.

The moon lodge comes from Native American culture where the women who were on their period go away from the village and go in the moon lodge. Our lodge was made of red fabric and it was like this spiral. Women who were not on their period served us and brought us food. Men are never allowed in, *ever!* Women who are bleeding are not to go in the sweat lodges, and women who are not bleeding don't get to come in the moon lodge.

There was straw on the floor and it was like this womb because it was red fabric and there was light coming in all the time. We would hang out. We'd sing a lot. We squatted on the ground and laid hands on each other's bellies and breathed. It was really cool. That was where I first got into cloth pads. There was a moon pot and you would put your pads in it after you were done. They would soak the blood into the water, then they would take the water and pour it outside into mother earth, which I still do. I like wearing cloth pads. I don't wear them during the day anymore because I bleed too heavily, but I wear them at night. It's worlds better.

There was also a simple initiation ritual where everyone got initiated into being a Maiden. I was the only person there who had just become a Maiden, most of these people were already Mothers or menopausal. I knelt down and they gave me a kiss on the forehead and gave me a gift and then I went to each of them. First I went to a Maiden, then I went to a Mother, then I went to a Queen, then I went to a Crone, and then it was over.

I think it's important to have a community of women because everybody accepts you. Women have their own set of things that come with their body, their own set of spiritual places, states that they can reach that men don't get to have. A lot of the root of that is the ability to bleed and the ability to bear children. This old Native American guy used to do healing energy work on my mom. Some Indian elders had given him the opportunity to experience what it's like having a period. He didn't actually have one but he felt it. He came out of it and he said, "How can you guys go to work? How can you even talk while this is happening?" We were like, "Well, if we didn't have to, we wouldn't."

Bleeding gives me the awareness of the cycles. It's not like a line or a flat plane. It's a cycle and you can come back. It's a spiral. Especially being a teenager and having all the hormones. You're up and you're down, then you come back up. You always come back up.

Having it monthly and being able to say, "Okay, I'm probably not gonna see any males on this day of the week of this month," is great. Usually right before or right on my period I avoid guys. I don't want their energy in my life right then.

Lately, as I'm seeing sexism in my life, I see how it affects people and how it makes them ashamed. I was not raised to being ashamed. If you are told all of your life that you're subordinate, that you're not worthy, that you're less than human, that your opinion is not valued, and that being a woman is something to be ashamed of, it'll screw you up pretty bad. It's a lot about worth. If you don't love yourself, you are incapable of completely loving anyone else. So take care of yourself and love yourself.

Linda Wolf and Wind Hughes talk with Barbara Walker

*B*arbara G. Walker is a pioneer in the women's spirituality movement and the author of dozens of books including The Woman's Encyclopedia of Myths and Secrets, The Skeptical Feminist, and The Crone.

Linda: Barbara, you've said to us that you believe all sexism stems from religion. Will you please tell us how you come to that conclusion?

Barbara: Everywhere in the world, sexist prejudice against women is associated with patriarchal religion - that is, religion in which the creator-deity is called 'he' and men are perceived as more like 'his' divine image than women are. Such religions usually have a creation myth something like the biblical one, claiming that man is created first and takes precedence over woman. Even claiming also that woman is somehow responsible for the existence of various evils such as sin and death.

These patriarchal religious myths falsely debase women and completely misrepresent their real function in humanity's early history/herstory. We now know - as biblical writers did not know - that human beings have lived on this planet for about three million years. It was only in the most recent five thousand years that human societies began to develop the notion of supreme father gods. Most primitive humans didn't know that there is such a thing as fatherhood any more than animals know it. Therefore, the principal creative deity almost certainly was the birth-giving Mother Goddess.

Women were revered as possessors of her sacred reproductive mysteries and the nurturers, teachers, lawmakers, and socializers of every child from its birth. The basic social unit was the maternal clan. We can see this kind of organization among the more intelligent social mammals such as elephants, whales, bonobos, and wolves. Not only fatherhood, but also war, violence, oppression, and intolerance seem to have been unknown to most early humans. So the modern, media-fostered view of a monogamous 'cave man' brutally mistreating a 'wife' and children (as too many civilized men do today) is quite wrong.

Wind: When did the father gods show up?

Barbara: When men began to realize that males have something to do with reproduction, they began to postulate father gods who could be begetters and therefore creators. Prior to that, the earliest gods were subordinate sons and consorts of the supreme Mother Goddess. Unfortunately, as human chieftains and kings identified themselves with these gods, they became greedy for temporal power and inflated their god-images to increase their own importance.

Eventually, in early Middle Eastern civilizations, the mother-clan system was abolished, usually by violence. God-endorsed systems of monogamy were instituted to make sure that each man could lay claim to his own children. It was believed that a father's comfort in the afterlife depended on having many children to worship his memory and divinize him. We see the biblical God promising this to his patriarchs (Genesis 17:6).

Unlike the ancient Mothers, patriarchal gods ruled by fear, threats, harsh punishments, and sadistic nightmares like the Christian vision of hell. To this day we hear the term 'God-fearing,' meaning a righteous person. Unfortunately, a spiritual diet of fear doesn't make people kinder or more generous. More often it makes them insecure, uptight, bigoted, and cruel. For the first time in two thousand years it's possible to re-habilitate the Mother

Goddess image as a spiritual symbol for girls and women who no longer need to relate themselves only to a concept of divine maleness.

Ritual, Ceremony, and Moon Lodges

Wind Hughes

With ceremonies and rituals we can make a moment or a day sacred, or honor something or someone important to us. They can be as elaborate as a Catholic mass or as simple as stopping on a path in the forest to place a flower on a stone while giving thanks for the beautiful day. Rituals are a natural expression of acknowledging and experiencing something greater than ourselves.

I've led and participated in many beautiful ceremonies. For the past six years I have been a member of a women's circle that meets on holy days (sabbats) and at other times to celebrate and honor events going on in our lives. We pray, meditate, dance, sing, and drum. We honor spirit, the seasons, nature ... any and every thing we hold special.

community, to share ceremony and celebrations with. A group of women on Bainbridge Island were feeling the same way. We got together and built a Moon Lodge for women and girls. We wanted a place to go to hold celebrations, a place to retreat and be alone to revitalize our connection to ourselves and the great mother, and a place to go when we were

I use ancient and traditional forms of ritual, but I also create my own ceremonies since rituals express what is in our own hearts and spirit. When creating a ritual, I spend time contemplating the person, the holy day, or the season it will celebrate. I try to discover what it means to me. What do I want to honor, ask for, or pray for? We can speak about our appreciation, ask for guidance or healing, or design a ritual to raise our consciousness.

For a time I missed having a group, a

bleeding on our moon cycle. It is a place of women's energy. No men can go there. When we want to share rituals with the men in our community, we do it somewhere else.

About thirty-five of us raised the money and built the Moon Lodge in the forest on a friend's property. It is a simple, round, canvas yurt on a wooden platform with a small deck in front. It's round because when I led the group on a guided journey, I had them close their eyes and picture what the Moon Lodge

Daughters of the Moon, Sisters of the Sun

should look like. When we opened our eyes, we drew what we saw and hung all the drawings on the wall. Even though many of the women had never seen a Moon Lodge, we weren't surprised to see that almost all of the drawings were of a round structure. We decided unanimously to make it round.

It took us a few months to design it, buy the lumber, and build it, and we had a great time doing it. Everyone did their share in some way. The floor is carpeted and the walls covered with beautiful cloth and tapestries. We have a wood-burning stove with a hearth/altar lovingly made of mosaic tiles inlaid with pieces of glass, old stones, shells, crystals, and beads in circular and spiral designs. We have abalone shells full of sage, cedar, and other herbs that we use for smudging - a simple ritual for cleansing and offering prayers. On the hearth/altar we've placed incense, candles, photographs, postcards, feathers, stones, poems, and even a vial of someone's menstrual blood.

A life-sized mannequin of a Crone, holding a staff, stands near the hearth. We made her, dressed her in elaborate clothes, and paraded her through the forest one night during a wonderful ritual honoring and celebrating the wisdom of older women. On one of the walls stands a six-foot fabric 'yoni' sculpture, symbolizing the vagina, to remind us of creation and the door to life. A journal is there for anyone to write in, and small instruments and drums are always around. Pillows and blankets are piled up against the wall and sometimes some of us spend a night or two there, warmed by the fire. It's a very special place.

Our lives have become so removed from experiences like these, and it is rare these days to have a community to share and celebrate with. I am so grateful for the friends and community that have grown here on this island and for the sacred celebrations we have shared together. The time that I take for ritual is special to me and helps me to remain awake and deeply aware of life.

I learned a lesson with this community of friends. It's easy to sit back and complain about what is missing in our lives. Instead of waiting for change to happen, we came together and created the change within ourselves and in our own community. When we join together with other like-minded souls, anything can happen.

Two

Taking it to the Edge

~

Suzanna Ribeiro

I was three or four years old the first time I said I didn't belong here. I was terrified of the dark and other people. I knew there were people out there who had a lot of pain and wanted to hurt others. I was afraid they would get me, but it was the darkness that scared me the most.

I went completely hysterical, totally out of control. I think that's how I ended up becoming anorexic. Not eating was something I could control. After that I wasn't afraid anymore. I think that's what happens in adolescence. You start to want to shrink away. What's weird now is that I've completely conquered my fear of the darkness and come around to where I celebrate it. I can see why I was so scared of it as a child - I had so much in me.

I first started dieting when my sexual hormones kicked in. I didn't like the way I looked and I didn't like that guys started noticing me. I was still afraid of people, but now I was afraid of my own sexual feelings, too. Not eating helped me withdraw into my own mind. I became seriously trapped inside myself, looking out, seeing people, yet not letting them get near me. By the time I was hospitalized, I had retreated so far behind my eyes that when I looked out I could see everybody, but their voices became more and more muffled.

I was very thin but I didn't think so. I weighed about ninety pounds. My face looked normal; my cheeks were red but my mouth was really big. I remember a girl saying that she thought I was so beautiful. I couldn't understand how people could think I was beautiful, and then I realized what they were seeing. I was this beautiful image of death - fragile, so skinny, and very pale except for my cheeks. I was like an untouchable, unreachable creature, a deadly nymph. It was confusing. All these people were saying I was beautiful while my experience was that I was dying.

I was tortured by food. I could not walk near the kitchen without walking around in circles saying, "I can't eat anything. I can't touch anything." I wanted to eat all the time. I thought I was eating all the time. I'd tell my mom I was but I'd probably be eating a lot of carrots or celery, so it only felt like I was eating all the time. I lost my period altogether.

To me, dieting and getting a man were the two most important things a woman could do. All the women's magazines said, "Seven New Ways To Lose Weight," "Fifteen Pounds Lost in Fifteen Days," or "How To Get Your Man." They influenced me to think losing weight was how I could get a man, how I could be a real woman. I wanted to get a man, yet at the same time I was also scared of my sexual feelings and I felt I shouldn't feel them. I don't think most young women ever learn that it's not wrong to have those feelings. It was okay for guys to go off and screw around with girls, but if girls did it they got a bad reputation.

What I most wanted was to look like a boy. No hips. Everything straight. I was so proud of myself. I had succeeded in looking like everyone wanted to look, but in order to reach my goal, I had to be starving and dying. Going without food is traumatic. You start hallucinating and thinking weird things. You don't realize how many chemicals are released by food in your brain. I thought about stopping, but it would mean eating and having sex again. Everything would go back out of control as it was before. There was no way to win. Finally it got so bad the doctor put me in the hospital. I was there for a month in a program for anorexic girls.

At first I didn't realize how depressed I was, but as they got me on Prozac I got better and then the hospital became a wonderful safe haven where there were others like me. They didn't look too skinny to me. The people who looked regular looked kind of fat to me. I don't know if being in treatment was the answer. You're in a safe place so far removed from the real world. You're protected from day-to-day reality. When my month was up I told my mother, "You want me to put on weight. I'll put on weight, but I have to stay here." I had come out from behind my eyes, but the glass of the hospital was as far as I wanted to go.

After I left the hospital, I went home and back to school. I was all right for a while. I felt good about my body and I had a lot of support. People would say, "Oh Suzanna, you look better every day," and that helped. I started to gain weight and my mom would take out my jeans without me knowing. I finished that year of school, had a great summer, and was regaining a new sense of innocence, and I could eat. But I met a boy and things started to change. I'd hear friends say that I looked just like his last girlfriend, "brown hair and skinny," and I'd think, "I have to stay that way or he won't like me anymore." Now that they got me eating, I couldn't stop. I was ravenous all the time, not just literally ravenous but sexually, too. I felt so full of everything, so full of life, but I couldn't let myself have it. I had to get it out of me. That's when I became bulimic.

I'd come home hungry after school, eat a big snack, and go, "Oh no, I had a snack and I'm still going to have to have dinner, too. I can't not eat dinner." I couldn't let my mom know I didn't want to eat anymore again. What would have been the point of her putting me through the hospital if I ended up not eating anymore? So I had to put up this image that, yes, I was eating. Yet I still had to stay skinny. It was all too much for me to handle. So I'd throw up. Every time I did it I'd feel better afterwards. I'd splash cold water on my face and swear that it would be the last time. I'd say, "I'm sorry, I'm sorry," but the next time I'd do it again. I'd always think, "Oh God, I did something bad. I'm a bad person." I'd start punishing myself.

Nobody knew I was doing it until, at the end of senior year, my mom found out. She came home early one day and walked in on me and said "Oh my God." That day I had hurt my throat so badly it was bleeding. My mom was so upset she left the house and said she wasn't coming back. She left quite a few times after that. I understand. She felt just as out of control as I did. When she found out I was bulimic, she didn't know what to do. I told her

I'd stop. I didn't stop. In fact, things got even worse. I started bingeing. I think bulimia is really bad because it gets your chemicals so wracked. It releases endorphins, so you get this high like doing drugs or something. Then you start having to do it because you deplete your body of so many nutrients that you have to eat again in order to feel okay, but once you start eating you can't stop making yourself throw up. It's a vicious circle. It's a constant feel good, feel bad, feel good.

The more I tried to control things, the more out of control I got. I didn't feel depressed, but now when I look back on it I am surprised I didn't try killing myself earlier. You feel trapped, yet it's such a comforting disease. It's like feeling good and bad and punishing yourself all in one, and it's like being withdrawn from everybody. It's a bigger secret than anorexia. With anorexia you can wear heavy clothes to make yourself look normal, but being bulimic requires you to plan things out in your head - where and when you can eat, where you're going to throw up.

When I was eighteen years old, I graduated from high school. I had been going through this since I was thirteen. I decided to take the year off and get a job. The bulimia was totally out of control by then and so was my sexuality. I slept around a lot. I got a lot of pleasure from the attention, but I didn't enjoy sex at all. I'd just do it because someone wanted me.

Bulimia ruled my life. I practically slept by the toilet bowl. I wanted to stop so badly that I started cutting my fingers each time I did it - to punish myself. My girlfriend Benny and I lived together in a cute little cabin. I could tell her a lot about my problems. She couldn't really help me, but she stuck with me anyway. We'd sit on our beds and I'd tell her who I would sleep with. Finally I came to a point where I felt I had to run away because I was sleeping with too many different guys.

On the road to California, I stopped eating and became anorexic again. By the time we got to California I was doing speed and acid. When I look back, all I see from that time are shades of gray. I'd go for six days straight without food. I lost my ability to articulate what was going on in my head. It was like I was being vacuumed in. People would talk to me, but I couldn't talk back.

When we got to Santa Barbara, I took a job at a deli and watched everybody else eat, but I wouldn't. I'd take things home so I could eat and throw up by myself. Around this time I got really obsessed with death. I was doing a lot of fighting in my head about saving myself and letting myself go. In my art I used Jesus and Satan as symbols – as my dark and light side. I liked the image of the devil because I felt that my bulimia was like the devil. I felt that every night he would come and take me over, this ugly creature. I had this art room; it was concrete and I started doing this piece on the wall. It was the devil and it said "Burn." I had this great idea of getting a gun and shooting myself with this great painting. I could see the forensic lab shots of the body beneath the sign saying "Burn" with the devil on it, and I thought it would be such a pretty picture, such a pretty way to go.

I was pretty fucking depressed by now and I knew it. I couldn't sleep and I didn't want to take showers anymore. Dying had become an obsession. I'd completed the painting and I wrote down what I was planning to do and when, but I couldn't get a gun. Every morning I'd wake up and ask myself, "Is this the day?" On April 9, I woke up and thought, "This is the day!" I forgot about it all day at work. I got home and I binged and threw up and it was like, "God I *really* can't do this anymore."

I went into the bedroom and got the sleeping pills. Once you start, it's just like one, two, three, and the next one and the next one and the next one and it's so easy. I took fourteen sleeping pills, half a bottle of painkillers, and then I took a shower and it was like, YES. I was the happiest, like being high, and I felt, "It's finally done with."

I think the reason I decided to do it then was because right before I took the pills, I imagined my funeral and I couldn't see anybody there. Before, when I'd think of death, I would ask myself if I could see anybody standing over my grave. I could see my mom and dad and my brother crying. For the most part, that's why I didn't kill myself. This time I couldn't see them so to me that meant I could go - that they let me go.

After my shower I lay down in bed. My house was a mess but I thought at least *I* was clean. I started to read a book and my heart skipped or something slipped and my whole body started to twitch and I thought, "Oh shit, I'm going to die twitching." That didn't fit my

pictures about a pretty death and I got scared. I started thinking, "I'm going to die here and who's going to find me? It's going to be Guilio." He was the old Italian guy where I worked. I could imagine him coming in saying, "Hey, Suzanna, Suzanna, wake up," and him trying to kick me awake and me being dead. I couldn't die like that with some old guy finding me. That's when I tried to call poison control. I was flipping through the white pages, the yellow pages, but it wasn't there. I tried calling friends. I'd tried calling them earlier, before I did it. I was pissed off now because I was out of control of my being able to kill myself, out of control of living or dying.

Just then the phone book kind of magically opened to the crisis center hotline, open twenty-four hours. I called and I asked if they had some information on overdosing. The woman on the other end said, "Um, well what did you take?" I told her and she said, "Holy shit, well okay, do you have anybody you can call?" I'm like, "I tried and nobody's there," and that's when I started going hysterical and she said "Calm down, calm down." So they called a cab for me. I don't understand how I walked out and locked my door and gave the cabby twenty dollars and walked into the hospital.

They pumped my stomach and they had to go up through my nose and down into my throat with this PVC piping, this big, long, cold tube. They put lubricating jelly on the end of it, stuck it up my nose, and at that point I was sitting straight up in the bed with four nurses having to hold me down 'cause I was just crazy. They kept on having to push harder and harder down my throat; that was the worst. All my reflexes were saying, "Get it out," and they were saying, "Suzanna, if you want to cooperate with this, you are going have to lay still," and I'm like, "Lay still? You try to have something shoved up your nose." It was so pathetic, it was so awful. Then they decided they had to put charcoal in me. I was cold already and I started going in and out of consciousness; they were afraid they were going to lose me. My veins had collapsed in my arms. They couldn't put an IV in me. I was at least half an hour with that tube in me, pumping out all the water and bile, and then it took extra time to get the charcoal in because it wasn't going in right. Removing the tube was just as bad as putting it in. I can hardly talk about it all now because I start to shake.

After it was all over and everybody left me alone, it was nice and quiet. I started thinking and that's where my life started turning around. I thought, "Okay, I've gone to death, I know what it's kinda like, and I can't really die right now because obviously if I didn't die this time there's a reason why." I finally got a hold of my mom. She was in South Carolina but she got me a plane ticket to stay with her. When I got there she was really angry with me. When you try killing yourself, you don't think about other people. People say it's the most selfish thing you can do, but that's because people who try to kill themselves can't see other people's reactions. Most people don't understand truly suicidal souls. My mom didn't give me any options. She told me I was going to move back home and get help. I think there was a certain point where she would have given up if I kept on doing bad stuff, but she wouldn't tell me when that would be. She'd just say, "We're going to do this for you and that for you and you have to stay home until you are on the right track."

Everything was out in the open. I started therapy and taking Prozac. Death seemed like something so beautiful and peaceful. Nobody could bug you any-more. There was a bigger part of me that wanted to die and a smaller part of me that wanted to live, but they shifted in their balance. I stopped wanting to kill myself.

I felt like I was being saved. It was nice to feel like a

kid again. I felt safe. Now there's a part of me that says, "I deserve to live and be happy," and the darker voice gets smaller and smaller. Still, sometimes when I get happy and relax and enjoy life, the darker side of me, the death side, comes up like a sweet song calling me and says, "You don't deserve happiness." I've worked hard in therapy. The structure keeping me alive is built around contracts I've made in therapy and with my mother. Rather than let the darkness overcome me, doing a lot of art-work helps me harness and embrace the dark-ness like a spiritual thing, like it's a part of me

and it's okay - integrating it.

When I see a teen or woman's magazine I get really mad and feel I'm not going to let the messages they project get me. It makes me stronger. I have to go kick some butt out there, get people shaped up, make sure girls don't have to go through what I had to go through. I'm sort of figuring out that I'm on a mission here. I can't kill myself, I can't let myself die. I have too much to do.

There's so much beauty in so many simple things. It's like reaching out and con-necting. The beauty is in each of us but we've been brainwashed into thinking that there is something more out there that we have to have. We're turned against each other - espe-cially women. Why are we are so turned against each other? It's like we are hypnotized and told there are barriers there, and we believe it. You have to be really open, and that's scary.

I've been feeling pretty free these days.

I'm a waitress in a great restaurant in the woods. My boyfriend Michael works there, too. Our relationship is really good. We were friends for quite a few years before we became lovers. For some reason I finally *got* how to have a relationship. He was my best friend and we used to talk all the time. We'd been through everything together. One day it dawned on me, "Wait a minute; he's the one I want to kiss - I want him to be close to me - I want to be with him." He's a good person to help shine the mirror in my face when I can't see myself.

My mission is about love right now, which is so contradictory to my wanting death. It's tough to know that you're here to spread love as well as to embrace the darkness and integrate it. Food is not an issue anymore, which blows my mind. I eat and I'm okay with my body. I like it for myself, I enjoy it. I still get really angry at the magazines. It sets a little fire under me every time I open them. I do it on purpose, too. I'll drag Mike to the magazine section and we open up the little girls' teen magazines and I tell him, "Rip out this page and this page, this we can do without, it's all bullshit."

We have to start as young as five and six, having young girls groups, so we can get used to being real with each other and know that we deserve being like this all the way through our teen years and all the changes. We have to break the glass and get out and tell the people we trust what's going on in our minds and bodies, tell them our secrets, even if we are afraid they'll be upset. They can, like my mom, pick us up out of the raging waters and save us. I know my life will keep on progressing through different stages, like it has already. I don't ever want to forget or cut out from my life what's happened to me. I'm just thankful I'm here now.

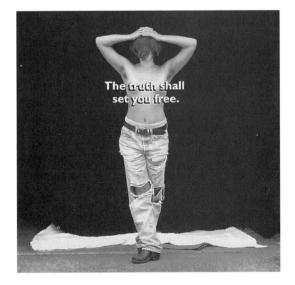

The truth shall set you free.

Dear Suzanna,

Thank you for sharing your story with me and with all who read this book, young and old. For some of us, your story echoes our own fear when we were attempting to make the transition into womanhood. We re-member in our bodies our sense of alienation, aloneness, hormonal conflicts, yearning for the fullness that food and sexuality and maturity seemed to promise. And yet, like you, we were aware of the false messages that we received from the media and family and friends. We felt caged and yearned for escape from life itself, as if that was the only way to freedom.

Thank you for staying on this side. Thank you for doing your artwork and writing and finding ways to relate to your mother and to Mike. These are your ways of finding a focus through to your own center. In finding your own truth through your own creativity and relationships, you are finding freedom. In his commonsense way, Christ puts it very succinctly: "The truth shall set you free."

Never give up, Suzanna. The journey becomes increasingly interesting - not necessarily easier, but more purposeful. Those of us who are acquainted with death can see the buttercups and hear the doves and experience life 'on the water' from a deep-down place of loving. Life becomes very precious in its tiniest details.

Live it, Suzanna. Stand tall in the beauty of your own womanhood. Whenever I am afraid, I say to myself, "I am a woman greatly loved and capable of great loving."

May love fill your being,

Marion Woodman
Toronto, 1996

Suzanna Ribeiro talks with Jean Kilbourne

*J*ean Kilbourne is a media critic and filmmaker who lectures on the effects of advertising on women and girls. Her upcoming book, Killing Us Softly: Romance & Rebellion in Advertising, will be published by Henry Holt & Company in 1998.

Suzanna: Jean, what was your childhood like? Were you anorexic or bulimic?

Jean: No, my compulsions were alcohol and cigarettes. As a child, I felt invisible. My mother died when I was nine years old. When I turned sixteen, things changed suddenly. I became quite visible because the world found me beautiful. I got a lot of pressure to capital-ize on my looks, so I modeled and participat-ed in beauty pageants, but I was very conflict-ed. It felt awful. In those days there was no feminist consciousness so when I said that it made me feel like a thing, nobody knew what I meant. I was always aware that being beautiful gave me an absurd amount of power but that it was short-lived and was going to be ruthlessly taken away from me as I grew older.

Suzanna: What helped you get yourself back into a healthy place?

Jean: When you're addicted to something, whether it be food or alcohol or whatever, it tends to take over your life and become a kind of higher power. I don't know any way to get beyond that without having a sense of something positive, good, that is more powerful than you are. It doesn't have to be God, but some force or nature that's positive. For me, in order to get free from alcohol, I had to give up the illusion that I was in control, live my life a day at a time, take care of myself, and connect honestly with other people.

Suzanna: In one of your videos you show a picture of a woman in a babydoll dress with her hair pinned up and you comment, "Does this woman look empowered?"

Jean: This is related to the fact that women are encouraged to look and be like little girls. And often real little girls are used in ads in sexy ways. Some people are afraid of grown-up and powerful women, so little girls become a substitute. People are terrified of a woman who is smart, equal, and in partnership with a man. We see that as unfeminine somehow.

Wind: Boys often say they don't need girls to look like the ideal image, but if you ask them to define what that is, they often describe what's on the cover of the magazines.

Jean: Girls are encouraged to achieve the ideal image and boys are encouraged to be successful, which means rich. They're pressured to look successful by having a woman or girl who has achieved the ideal on their arm.

Suzanna: Here in the United States, the ideal image is to be skinny, yet we have the highest percentage of overweight people and heart disease in the world.

Jean: We get a lot of double messages. We know that to be healthy we should exercise and eat wholesome, balanced foods, yet fast-food places are everywhere. We're encouraged to eat junk food and watch lots of television. Worse, the emphasis is not on exercising to be fit but on how many calories you can burn off.

I'd love to see the emphasis on other goals. Playing a team sport or tennis or taking a walk through the woods, just being active. I hate that the goal for women is simply to be good-looking, decorative sex objects, and for our bodies to be useful to men, not to ourselves.

But the issue with thinness is a separate issue. The pressure on girls and women to be very thin has a lot to do with fear of power in women, fear of women taking up too much space.

Suzanna: Whenever we go into the supermarket, I drag my boyfriend over to the magazine stand and start ranting. Is there any way to combat these images besides not buying the magazines?

Jean: Yes, I think there are lots of ways and one is to do just what you're doing. People are unconscious of the influence these images have on our lives. Once they're conscious, they have more power to resist them. Of course it's sometimes a good thing to boycott products and write letters, but most of all we have to be educated. We have to teach media literacy in school, starting in kindergarten. Teach kids to be critical viewers so that they won't be so taken in by these messages.

There's no simple answer. There's always been a cultural standard of beauty, but it hasn't always been the same standard, nor has everyone been pressured to achieve it. Until recently, the standard had to do with fuller bodies, where the underlying value was fertility. Ample hips, round stomachs, big breasts, like the fertility goddesses. Today the ideal is a sort of antifertility symbol where, in the majority of cases, the model has ceased to menstruate because she is so thin. Education is important, bringing these things out in the open, consciousness-raising, getting people to see that the ideal changes over time and across cultures.

We have to do something about the ownership of the media. Recently, the U.S. Congress deregulated the media to the extent that a handful of men now control almost all the newspapers and magazines, television and radio stations. That's a very dangerous situation. We have to demand of our elected officials that we diversify the ownership of the media. We're heading into a situation where we're going to end up with a half dozen corporations which will control virtually everything. Then you get a merger like Time/Warner and *Time* does a review of a Warner movie. When General Electric owns a television network, how likely are we to get any hard-hitting investigations of the defence industry? There are groups trying to fight back. The Cultural

Environment Movement is one. They specifically address who owns the airwaves and how we can get them back. That goes way beyond the problem with image. That gets into the question of what is the 'news' and how do we get information?

Suzanna: What else can we do to help ourselves and each other?

Jean: It's so important to share our experience with each other. People need to realize that anorexia and bulimia are major public health issues. We have to break through the denial, deglamorize extreme thinness, and recognize it for the problem that it is, and get the information out about how people can get help. Anything we can do to strengthen our friendships with each other, cross-generationally and with our mothers, goes a long way to help us feel not so alone and isolated and increases our self-esteem. We need private discussion groups and books like this, ways to see ourselves as allies.

Also, we need to stop being so hard on each other if we do go for the glamor. I like to think of this period as an interim time, as we sort all these things out. There are a lot of actresses who have cosmetic surgery as they grow older. It's easy to say, "Oh, they should grow old gracefully," but if it means that they aren't going to get any more parts, then it's worth it to keep the acting going. We need to be less critical of each other, not more critical, with whatever choices we make, and realize that feminists can look many different ways, can choose many different styles. We shouldn't be questioning someone's sincerity based on that. For a while, when I started lecturing in public, I didn't shave my legs or shave under my arms, but after a point the grief wasn't worth it. I had to fight so much harder to get my message across through the screen of people's projections onto me that I decided not to fight that battle. I don't think it's hypocrisy; it's just what works. If we want to get our messages across, we can't scream at people. They won't hear what we have to say – and the important thing is to have people hear us.

McKayla Hauschulz

I've always been a bit eccentric. In school, people think that I'm being myself, but I don't really know who that self is. I dress for other people rather than dressing for me. I think it has to do with the fact that I'm so used to being on stage or being on display and having other people watch me. I've been acting since before I can remember. Clothes are just costumes for me.*

Sometimes I get a glimpse of McKayla. I guess she is a bit of all the parts I play. Sometimes she's the fairy queen, sometimes she's beatnik, sometimes she's hippie, sometimes she's punk, and sometimes she's blues. She's very into trying out new things and she doesn't really know where she fits in yet, or if she fits in at all. She's a chameleon, adapting to wherever she is, whoever she's talking to, whatever she's wearing.

When I am alone I feel more comfortable, I can be me, but put me in a social situation and it's different. I'm like the walls in my room; each one is different. I used to have my Drew Barrymore wall all covered in her pictures, and my wall that was covered in fairy pictures, and one that was plastered in my poetry and pictures. But I stripped them all down because I didn't want their reflections staring back at me anymore. Now one is blank, one is covered with aluminum foil, and the other has a Casablanca poster.

I first realized I was suicidal last year when I was a sophomore. I would prick my fingers with needles and let myself bleed and scratch messages in blood. It didn't hurt. It felt good, like the old medieval idea of bleed-ing out a disease – like I could bleed myself of whatever was hurting me. I did it alone a few times, but I mostly did it with other people. We'd be like, "Oh there's nothing to do; math class is boring today so let's go slice our fingers and bleed." I never did it as much or as badly as some girls I know. I think people would be amazed at how many girls do it. I'd also write suicide notes, which I'd never send, and do crazy things like bang my head against the wall and scream really loudly and take all kinds of pills. I never knew who I was angry at besides myself. It was like I had this evil twin sister looking at me from the mirror, trying to get me to come over to her side and do what I'm not supposed to do. I called her Ivy. She's this dark girl with dark hair, not at all like a teenager. She doesn't twist around the truth. She's blunt. She says things like, "Come on, you know you hate yourself, you know you hate life, you know you hate everything, you know you look like shit, you know you feel like shit, you know everyone hates you, you know you're a failure. Why don't you just come with me? Because they're never going to love you and they're never going to respect you and they're never going to give you what I can give you, because I understand you and they don't. You might as well just die."

I've thought about how to heal her sometimes. I'd have her fall in love. I'd have her meet someone she could trust, someone who could hold her when she's the darkest and still love her. But she won't call out for help. She's not the type to call people when she's down; it's not her style. She needs people to call her.

I haven't killed myself because I haven't gone through anything serious enough where I would actually want to. I mean, I've been on the verge and I've been over the edge a lot, but I never expected to die. I just wanted to get away from everything for a while. I talked with my mom a few times about it, nothing really serious. I talked about maybe getting into therapy or getting some sort of help. I didn't tell her the full extent of my feelings because I didn't feel there was any way she would help and I felt if she tried to, it would push me further over the edge. I felt I needed to figure things out for myself. I wanted someone outside of my life who didn't know me, who had no idea where I'd come from, who had no preconceived ideas, who wouldn't judge me - like a therapist. It's hard for me to

talk to people because I've been betrayed so many times. Not really betrayed, but they'd tell other people and I can't deal with that.

I'm a really hard person to deal with

because of my mood swings. I go through times when I'm happy and ecstatic to see everyone, the sweetest little thing in the world. I give everyone presents and am their best friend and two days later I won't talk to anyone and just constantly bitch about everything and do really mean things. I don't know how any of my friends stay friends with me – actually most of them aren't at this moment. For a while I thought it was PMS, but I'll be down for periods of three months and then be up for two weeks and be down again for six months.

When I'm down I don't want to talk to anyone; I feel disconnected from everything. People say hello to me and I ignore them or say whatever I have to to get them off my back. I feel like no one understands or cares about what I feel. I think they're all superficial - just doing what I'm doing: going about their lives; trying to get people off their back; dealing with other people so they don't *really* have to deal with them. In school, the question everyone asks twenty times a day is, "How are you?" but they don't really care. It's just a way of saying "Hey."

The responsibilities and requirements of school put too much pressure on me. It's the pressure to get good grades and fit in. Even if you say you don't want to fit in or even if people think you don't want to, you still have to because that's the way society works. You have friends' expectations of you. They hint the expectations; they don't say them in so many words. No one's honest. No one knows what they want. No one knows anything. They take you places and expect you to do things. Like you'll go to parties and everyone will be smoking pot and they'll expect you to. They'll

tell you their whole life history, absolutely everything that's wrong with their life, and expect you to feel pity or turn around and tell yours. They're experimenting with different levels of relationships and what they want from different people.

When I'm eighteen, I'm moving to Hollywood to work as a waitress in a diner or in a thrift store and maybe work as a table dancer once a week and write a hell of a lot of poetry on the side. What interests me about table dancing is that it's all about desire, lust, and passion but without the emotional connection. Plus there's the money and the fact that you get to dance. I'd rather be a stripper, though, because that leaves more up to the imagination and it's more seductive. Seduction is enticing to me because then I'll know I'm really wanted.

Sex is where I've gotten the most attention in my life, in my interactions and in the feedback I get from other people, my friends, even if they mean it in a good way, just all the people I know, so I think it's the only way I can connect with people and feel people connect with me.

Children are the only people I form

healthy relationships with because they are real. They look at the world and tell it like it is. They don't have underlying motives like teenagers. Teenagers will sneak around to get what they want; children are like, "Can I have that?" I can trust them; they're honest. They don't play you off of someone else because they haven't experienced that yet. Children don't hold on to the way you were the day before. They're immediate. With teenagers, if I'm depressed one day and happy the next, they'll be like, "Why are you so happy today? Yesterday you were all depressed - what happened?" If I could have relationships with teenagers like I do with children, it would be great. Children believe everything; teenagers doubt everything. Children have an open heart; the older we get, the more closed it becomes.

I could say I want to grow up, but I don't. I feel like if someone took me to a psychiatric ward, that would be beneficial to me. I don't know. Actually, I think I'd really like to be in a rehab place where there are always people there, like constant surveillance, like a healing center. I think that would be very good for me, because I could dig deeper in myself than I could alone.

For the most part, I've never felt wanted. Not even by my parents. They were loving, caring, affectionate, helpful, encouraging, but I never really felt wanted. It's just me. I don't know why. I don't feel that there's anyone who really cares about me. I don't feel like there's anyone I can talk to when I'm blue. No one stable enough that's within reach. Not even my mother. She's busy and I don't want to make her cry again, I don't want to burden her. Even if she told me she wanted me to burden her, I would think she was lying because she has too much to deal with and I just don't feel important. It's just that I want someone to love me completely with every morsel of their soul, forever.

If I were to give advice to someone like me, I'd say, "If you're hurting yourself mentally or physically, tell someone. If you're believing things about yourself that aren't true - like that you're ugly or not smart or that you'll never amount to anything - if you feel there's no one you can tell, at least find some way to express it, acknowledge it. Write. Paint. Act. Read. Anything. And if you do get to the point of physical harm, get into therapy or at least find some way to deal with it. Don't isolate yourself. Tell someone."

The truth is, if I wrote this story tomorrow, it would all be different. I'd probably still be saying the same things, but I'd come up with different reasons for it. The truth is, je ne sais pas. I'll tell you one thing that's true though: butterflies are free!

McKayla Hauschulz talks with Lindsay Wagner

Lindsay Wagner makes little distinction between her roles as an actress, advocate, mother, humanitarian, or author. What unites these various parts is a commitment through her work and her personal life to advancing human potential.

McKayla: How has acting helped your life?

Lindsay: I started taking acting classes when I was twelve. It turned out to be sort of like therapy for me. In those days, the more pain I was in, the more jokes I told. I couldn't share my pain *directly* with anyone. I always felt like that would be a burden. I was working on a good case of ulcers from the time I was fourteen until I was twenty. I was eating myself up with the things I was afraid to let people see.

When I started acting, it was incredible. It was like someone had taken a knife and lanced this huge swollen wound inside me. Finally I had a place where I could express my pain and I felt safe because I didn't have to put my name on it. I think acting kept me alive back then.

Something else happened when I shared myself through those characters; I saw people benefit from it. They thanked me and that really meant something to me. It was the first time I thought maybe there was something good about sharing my pain.

McKayla: Besides acting, what else has helped you in dealing with your pain and healing?

Lindsay: I've experienced several different healing methodologies over the years - counseling, self-help seminars, and I've read a lot - but none of them will work unless you really want to heal. A lot of people say they want to get out of pain, and I'm sure that's true, but they aren't willing to make healing a high priority. They aren't willing to look inside to see the source of their pain in order to deal with it.

I have always had a strong spiritual life. That's not to say I didn't spend a few years, when I was a teenager, cut off from my experience of that reality. I remember feeling so hurt once I said, "God, how can you be good if you let all these bad things happen? I don't want to talk to you anymore." But by the time I was sixteen, I'd sorted out that it wasn't God's fault people acted the way they did. He/She was waiting for people to wake up, to stop indulging in their fear/control games, and to start using their will to choose to be open to learning instead of protecting themselves. What a different world it would be if people did that! I also realized I didn't have to understand everything in order to ask for help from the source of all life, the source of love.

So I would ask for strength, guidance, healing, clarity, something constructive that would bring me joy. I just kept asking and opening myself to receiving help. I still do. The tough part of that process is not to get a fixed idea on how you want the help. You can be given a better solution than you could have imagined, or the first step in an even bigger healing process, but you look right by it because you're looking for the answer the way you think it should be.

Once you go inside and weed through the muck, you will find the real beauty, the truth about yourself. Then no matter what goes on around you in the physical universe, hang on to what you know. No matter who rejects you, don't lose touch with your higher self, with the higher powers, with anything that you can find which is of the light, that will give you strength in those times when you feel so lonely. That's the only way I have made it through. And when you're stuck and you can't get any farther by yourself, you've got to use your *will* to reach out for help. If the person you ask can't help you, reach somewhere else. Of course the best kind of help is the kind that helps you find the truth inside yourself again.

When I was younger, there were times when I was in so much pain I would lock myself away for days, never telling a soul. Finally, one friend I had, through relentless love, got through to me. She would barge in when I was all locked away and say, "This is not acceptable, what's going on?" But you can't always make it somebody else's responsibility to come get you. At some point you have got to take responsibility for saying, "Okay, I'm doing it again. I'm locked away," and use your will to reach out for help. I would experience terror trying to reach out. I'd ask myself, "What's the big deal? Why can't I call? Why can't I tell someone?" Finally I'd get the guts to call my friend. Afterwards, I'd be so embarrassed that I even had to ask for help and I was mortified that she had seen me in a fragile condition. Then I'd cry and then we'd laugh and it would be over and I'd go, "That wasn't so bad, what the heck was I so afraid about?" But I'd go through those same feelings again, every time. Eventually it got easier and easier, and through that relationship I learned to do in life what I learned to do through my work.

Look at Mother Nature, all the things we do to her. We slap cement all over her, yet, through the tiniest crack in that cement, something will grow. That's the nature of God, the Creator, Wakan Tanka, whatever you want to call it. All we have to do, when we get solidified by our negative emotions, like cement over a growing thing, is use our will to make those cracks. Have the guts to make the tiniest crack and let that source come through with new life.

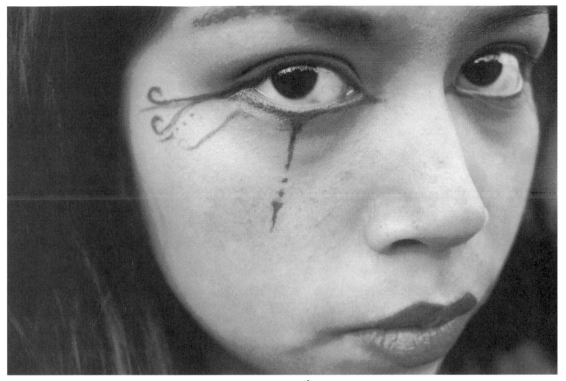

Eeah

My name is Eeah. I'm seventeen. I live in Suquamish with my mother, brother, and stepfather.

I was born in Forks, Washington, near our reservation in Neah Bay. We were pretty poor. We lived in what was basically a shack. It's not like we didn't have enough food; it's just that on the Makah Reservation, like on most reservations, people don't have much work or enough to do. We moved to Seattle when I was two, but we got robbed so many times we decided to move to Bainbridge where my grandparents had a farm. It was okay there, but I didn't fit in. In Seattle I was a tomboy who played in the dirt and beat up kids. The Bainbridge girls were into Barbie dolls and the boys didn't play with girls. So I spent most of my time with my cousins. Practically everybody dark was my cousin. When I was twelve, my parents divorced. When my mother remarried, she got the American dream. My stepdad is white and they both work on the ferries and for the first time we live in a nice house.

I don't really remember when I first started smoking pot. I grew up knowing the smell because it was always around. Probably my cousins first turned me on to it. They turned me on to drinking. But when I was thirteen, I had this secret identity. I lived in this trailer outside our house so I could sneak out all night long. I never told anybody - my parents still don't know - but I'd sneak out every other weekend, do Ecstasy, and go to raves. I'd go with this guy I met at a party in Seattle. He was eighteen. We'd get stoned and he'd give me this pill and I'd take it without any questions.

I really got into the music. It was a kind of techno. There's lots of types of rave music: there's house, hard house, jungle, ambient, trance, and other types. It's mixed on two turntables by a DJ who makes it up as he or she goes along. They'll puts songs together and makes a whole different one. They do that for eight hours straight, with no breaks. So it sounds like one droned-out musical journey of weird sounds and beats.

When I was younger, raves were just about dancing, doing drugs, and having a good time, but when I got older, I realized they were about a celebration of knowing. After Ecstasy, I'd started doing acid and realized that there was more to life than just having fun, that there was a deeper meaning to things. In general I felt depressed and lost, needing to know where I was going and what I was doing, and it's like acid put a mirror up to my face. I kept taking more and more because I knew it was opening up doors I needed to open, yet I was confused by what I was starting to see. I felt like there was a big empty space in what I knew about myself. I knew there was more, but I didn't know what. In some ways I was searching hopelessly.

Looking back, I'm so glad I went through that period. If I hadn't done acid, I wouldn't be where I am now, and right now I'm pretty happy. Well, comparatively, considering all the things that are happening around me. If I didn't do drugs, I wouldn't be able to handle life right now because when I'm on drugs, I look at the symbolism in life. Drugs have helped me to understand a deeper level of life. When hardships come, they're easier to handle because I realize that life goes on and I just have to keep it together. Plus, I feel like I have a purpose now.

I remember the feeling I had the day I realized this. I was with a friend and we schroomed in the morning and went to the hemp fest on the Island. At a certain point I decided to go home, but I had to catch the bus. I started peeking at the bus stop and I couldn't figure out the schedule so I went down to the waterfront and started crying for no reason. I had a really strong feeling that I'd stepped into something else, that I completely forgot the old me, that I forgot how to be myself and was a completely different person. I figured out how to catch the bus and on the whole bus ride home I cried, thinking that I couldn't have the same friends I had because they didn't know what I knew. I kept asking myself what I knew that was so strong to change me so completely. I laid in bed for five hours, really high on this feeling, thinking all the time that I couldn't be friends with all the same people. I'd lose everybody because of what I knew.

A couple weeks later I did acid with some friends. They were playing a game where they tried to explain what life was like to a hula hoop. They were talking in symbolism, making sense but not really. They kept using the word *it*. A few weeks later I fried by myself and kept thinking back on that night and I figured out what *it* was. I saw *it* was me, *it* was everybody, *it's* one, *it's* everything, *it's* the soul, *it's* spirituality, *it's* the knowing of all knowings, *it's* the stream of consciousness, *it's* all the words you can put to it, but *it* is the word for me. I felt like I found my purpose and that was to show *it* to other people. Since then I have helped about eight other people find it: their spiritual center, their path, their soul, their oneness. The value of knowing *it* is that it makes you realize that the meaning of life is simply to be. To be in the moment.

It's easy for me to see when somebody is lost and having a hard time trying to find themselves. I know they want to stop suffering. I see myself as a psychedelic shaman. I can't do it with sober people though, because they aren't completely open. They're bogged down and worried. But when someone is in an altered state of mind, it's really easy to open them up and show them.

It's like the waking state of consciousness we're in is really a state where we are asleep. I think we're born wide open but we're taught to be blind. When we're children, we look at the world totally differently. We are in the moment. Just being. When we get older we're taught to be socialized. We get self-conscious. We're supposed to be socially acceptable, to conform and do things to succeed. We're taught that success isn't in who you are; success is in what you do. It makes us stop wanting to be open with people and show them who we really are. We end up showing them what we can do instead.

You probably wonder what my life is like now that I know all this. I think I get along fine. Right now I live with my mom and stepdad, but if I had to be out on my own, I'd get a menial job if I had to. I'd find roommates and do the basic things I'd have to do to eat and live, but I'm not really a career-oriented person. The core of my happiness isn't to go out and make money. Knowing exactly who I am, knowing I don't have to do things people tell me I should do, knowing I can find other people who know - that's what's important to me. I just want to be fully aware whatever I do; even washing dishes can be done consciously.

People ask me how I see my future. I never really think about that anymore. I imagine that when I'm twenty-five I'll probably be a lot older than most twenty-five-year-olds. I know I'll know so much more than I know now. I'm just trying to figure out how to live in the world with what I know. I want to be a DJ for raves, but it takes a lot of money to buy the record players, speakers, mixers, and records. I think it will be one of my best investments if I can. I don't worry about my social life. I look at people as people. I see intimacy as part of my future, but I don't imagine getting married. I would be considered bi because I like boys and girls. I can never see myself getting married with a white dress and a big church. I can't imagine seeing myself having kids. I used to say I needed help. But the help I was looking for I found in me. Nobody else could show me.

June 1997

It's been over a year since I wrote the piece above. Since then, my views on the use of mind-altering substances have changed. Recently, I've become aware that it is very difficult to communicate with others where I have been, and that leaves me in a place of feeling alone with everything I have to deal with. Also, I have realized that balance and connection with others should always come before "realizations." One thing my experiences with drugs have contributed to, though, is that I feel I have conquered my fear of the depths in darkness and light, as well as my fear of the powers of the mind, which seem to be endless. I have found that anything is possible as long as the mind hangs on to its imagination, dreams and fantasies. It is completely evident to me that we are our own gods - just like in nature, we create who we are and destroy who we once were.

I do not believe that drugs created these views. It is me who learned how to properly use the alteration of my own mind to discover itself. I understand the differences between use and abuse of drugs. I see that the drug problem in society is a cause for fear. But I also believe that this problem is being dealt with without understanding, and that society has contributed to the problem getting out of hand. People need to acknowledge that it is part of human nature to want to constantly grow and evolve, as well as to want to escape. But for me, personally, what it comes down to is that, while I neither advocate nor condemn the use of drugs, I do not deny or regret where they have taken me. Still, right now, I've made the decision to slowly but surely wean myself away from the use of drugs because I no longer feel the need to intensify what is already constantly intense, and also out of respect for the Native name I will be receiving from my family in a sacred ceremony they're giving me soon.

Eeah and Wind Hughes talk with Anisa Romero

*A*nisa Romero is the lead singer for the *Seattle band* Sky Cries Mary. *She is also an accomplished painter and a world traveler.*

Wind: Your music is very psychedelic, yet my sense is that you don't do drugs. Is that true?

Anisa: Everyone in the band has experimented with drugs, but we decided a few years ago, after one of our band members kicked heroin, that when we practice and do shows, there are no drugs, there's nothing. It's out of respect for everyone else. We found that we could reach those same kinds of highs and levels and oneness by doing our art, and we all saw how empowering that was. Personally, I drink a little wine, but that's it. I think there's a profound natural high in the universe that you can tap into through art and yoga, natural highs that are part of ancient traditions of soul-searching. Drugs can definitely get you there, but they're a shortcut.

I lived in an ashram for a while and people would ask the swami if samadhi or enlightenment is similar to taking acid or mushrooms. He thought drugs were a good way for westerners to get there because that's how our culture is: we're kind of a junk-food culture. Fast food, fast enlightenment. You can use drugs as a tool to make you realize that there's something beyond our normal perceptions, but you won't get the whole picture.

Wind: Being in the music industry, have you struggled with your ego?

Anisa: It's definitely hard. I think you have to separate yourself from your art and let it be its own entity. When I was studying Eastern philosophy, the big question was whether we had to do away with the ego to feel oneness with everything. I think it's a struggle for everyone. I've got an ego. It's hard for me if we get a bad review.

Eeah: I'm really trying to be a DJ, and what I'm trying to get over is the ego. Some DJs put down other people. They think they're better.

Anisa: If you want to be a DJ, you just need to start doing it. Have you started?

Eeah: I've got *lots* of records, but I don't have turntables so I don't get to practice very much. I know eventually I'll make it there, but it's so slow. It's hard to express my feelings in words. It's hard to communicate. I've been going inward lately. Thinking about life and death. I'm not worried about it. I don't fear death. I accept it as part of life.

Anisa: Just looking death in the eye, accepting that it is present at all times, made me enjoy my life. It made me realize that our time is limited and there's not much time to be

wasted. You have to start doing what you want to do, no matter what. I had cancer in 1986. I'm still suffering from the consequences of the treatments and the operations, but it really directed my life.

I started college the same year. I became immediately focused and said, "I wanna be an artist. I wanna paint. I wanna sing." So I approached college with a different viewpoint than most people. I was studying what I wanted to know and what I wanted to learn, and there was no reason that I should study anything else because ... why would you? You've got one life. Cancer focused me and made me appreciate what I have.

Eeah: I know what I want, but real things are holding me back, the stupid little things that I can't change any faster. Like living at home, not having a car, and having a low-paying job. Just the simple day-to-day things. That part of my life moves really, really slow.

Anisa: There're always obstacles in the way - always, always, always. What you're gonna do and how you're gonna do it is completely your own decision. I think fear is the ultimate enemy. Fear always creeps up: should I do this, how am I going to do this, or will I be criticized for that? But you're not going to know until you do it. So if you experience fear, look it in the eye and plow forward.

Wind: Can you talk about techno music?

Eeah: Techno furthers people's knowledge without actually having to say anything. It shows them that there's so much more out there. There are sounds to be discovered. Sounds you've never heard before and wouldn't anywhere else. Even if you use traditional instruments, you can play with the sound and completely change it into something new. And that's what techno keeps doing. It reinvents itself over and over again. I think it's one of the fastest progressing sounds.

Anisa: People say it's the death of music, but I think it has become its own art form because, just like Eeah was saying, you can take a sound that someone else created on the other side of the planet and you can completely change it. You can add reverbs, echoes, slow it down or speed it up, or add something else, so definitely it's become its own art form. With

Sky Cries Mary, we like to use everything - real instruments, synthesizers, samples. We've experimented with all of it, kind of like with spirituality. You read about a Catholic saint or a Hindu saint or a South African goddess and take what applies and makes sense to you. Then it becomes your own.

Wind: You are well educated. How do you view the importance of education?

Anisa: I'm always educating myself, always reading and trying to learn more. Knowledge is power. It's important not to lock yourself into a dogma and think that you've figured it all out. The answer is always changing. We're always different people from one minute to the next. Education is everything. The most important thing is to follow your heart and try to do everything in a mindful way, every action you take. Keep reading and listening to things that inspire you. Do whatever it takes to keep in touch with what you love and the reason that you're here and what you want to do with yourself, and give back to the Earth for your life.

Erin Eychaner

*P*rior *to treatment, these were my words: "I just want to say that I'm never more alive than when I'm on three hits of acid. I feel like I'm on the edge and alive. I get out of my body and feel disconnected and free. If it were around all the time, I'd probably do it every day."*

I'd go on, "Adults just don't understand. When we say we're doing drugs, they think we're smoking crack in the alley, pulling needles from under the mattress. They don't understand that on acid we're loving everything, like being in the forest and merging with nature. For me, being a teenager is a phase of life where you can do really crazy things and get away with it. When you're a teenager, everything is provided for you. I have a roof, I have food, I have a home to go home to, I don't pay taxes. What better time than this to do everything I can do?"

I was always considered the problem child of the family, and I think I was fulfilling that role to the best of my abilities. It was an easy way of not having to put a whole lot of effort into living. I felt, "If this is what they think of me, then why not do this?" I was always a moody child with huge emotional swings. I didn't want them to be disappointed in me. But at the same time, I didn't want to try and improve my image of myself in their eyes. I just didn't want to be around them. I just didn't want them in my life.

It was a depressing period. I was constantly surrounded by people, but at the same time it was really lonely. I wasn't happy about where I was, what I was doing, or who I was with. I didn't know what I wanted to do. By doing things like acid and constantly having fun, I wouldn't have to think about what I was doing with myself. I was corroding relation-ships with my family and I came very close to destroying my scholastic career. Very close. I didn't want to have to face the repercussions of that or the reality of that.

Mainly I was just smoking a lot of bowls throughout the day. It was just habit. Something I did and didn't think about it. There's a lot of spirituality when it comes to using drugs. I think you get some of it whether or not you're searching for that while using them. You lose connection with your body regardless. Because your body doesn't know what's going on and it's *very* much a mental thing. And there's definitely the allure of feeling disconnected and free. You're not grounded and you're not weighed down.

There was one weekend in particular where I lost my job, I had been officially thrown out of school, and I'd been thrown out of my mom's house. It was a really bad weekend for me. After that I realized, "This isn't fun anymore. I don't have any place to go after school. I don't even go to school. I don't have any place to go to be alone."

Now my family is probably the most important thing in my life. At that time, none of them wanted to have anything to do with me. I couldn't even get along with my older sister anymore, which said a lot because she and I were very close. I was constantly lying to them, and you don't want to lie to people you care about. But once you start, it's this huge web, and you have to keep covering your tracks. It wasn't easy anymore. I was lying about where I was, who I was with, what I was doing while I was with them. If you can't tell people what you're doing, then there's something wrong there.

I ran away several times after that weekend. I'd go to school and see who wasn't going to classes that day, and then I'd spend the day with them. I was looking for things to fill up my time. Some older friends rented a house. It was the easiest place to go because there weren't any parents there who would be asking questions. Nobody was concerned about me there. I rarely paid for any drugs. Friends bought them. Nobody wants to do drugs alone, and I was somebody who was always willing to do that with them, so they always came to me. If anybody was gonna be at a party, I was gonna be there. I was really good company.

My dad wanted me to be checked out for clinical depression. I was getting to know this counselor and letting her know what was going on in my life on a regular basis, and she flat-out said to me, "I can't tell you whether or not you're clinically depressed until you're off drugs." So she asked me to take a drug evaluation test and I agreed to do it. I had never taken a test like that before, and I didn't know they could do anything about it. So I took the test, and they decided that I was a first-degree addict or something along those lines. I don't remember what the term was. In their eyes it was either get me to a treatment center now or I was going to die. Which wasn't true. I wouldn't have died, but my life certainly wasn't going well.

I agreed to go to treatment in Bellingham, not because I wanted to stop doing drugs but because it was another easy thing to do. It was free room and board. I didn't have to go anywhere for a month straight. It was a quick fix-it as far as I was concerned.

I saw a lot of hard-core drug addicts and I realized that I was very close to being like them, if not already so, and I didn't want to end up that way. Through the work that they have you do, you learn so much about yourself, whether you want to or not. You may think you're having a regular conversation with the counselors; you're out there, you're smoking your cigarettes, you're waiting for dinner to start, and they'll be sitting there talking to you, and the next thing you know you're getting this huge lesson on life without even meaning to. It was a great experience. I don't want to go back, but I really enjoyed it.

The counselors are all recovering drug addicts or recovering alcoholics, and just listening to how they turned their lives around and how much happier they are now was great. I aspire to be like them. There are a lot of hard drugs out there and a lot of really desperate people who are using them. I realized that I was heading in the wrong direction if I wanted to be a happy, content person. I wasn't going about it quite the right way, and they helped me realize that. I don't think I completely hit rock bottom, but I definitely hit a bottom of sorts. It could have been a lot worse than it was. At least for me it was enough of a bottom to make me realize that I was unhappy. I was sick and I didn't want to continue living my life that way.

The counselors work through the 12-step program. They take you by the hand and they walk you through it and ask you questions about what's going on. I realized that what's happened is in the past, is over. You need to let it go and that was a difficult thing to do. I had my whole life in *front* of me, and I didn't need to be continuously living in the past. In treatment I only had myself, so I had to reestablish that connection with myself in order just to be there. A treatment center is a very negative, hard place to be. You're surrounded by a group of kids who don't want to be there and they're miserable in their life. I didn't feel like I could really lean on them and depend on their strengths because they didn't have any, and if they did have them, they didn't have enough to share or to carry anybody else. You have to carry yourself.

When I finished the program, I had the option of staying in that town and getting a job and starting life all over again, or moving back in with my parents, which I didn't want to do. I knew that if I did go back and start seeing the same friends that I had been seeing, the same thing would happen all over again. So I stayed in Bellingham. I felt, "The whole world is for me and I'm here to play in it." I've really enjoyed being on my own, and not being at home has helped me be able to reestablish a relationship with my parents, without the constant head butting, because I'm not there all the time.

When I did go home and visit my friends, it was awkward. I think they were intimidated by me because I had grown into an entirely different person. They probably felt I didn't approve of what they were doing and that I looked down on them, which I didn't. I just felt concerned about them. It took a lot for me to feel like they trusted me again. If you care about somebody, that feeling's not just gonna go away because they've left the town and done something else with their life. If you care about somebody, you care about them and you're willing to work through things.

One of the main problems with drug abuse is you're compromising yourself on many, many different levels. You're compromising your values, your health, and your stability. There's a thin line between using and abusing. I know people who you don't want to talk to until they've taken a hit off of their pipe in the morning. That's the first thing they need to do in order to get through the day. To me, that's abuse. If you need it as a survival tool, if you're dependent on it in order to cope with other people and cope with the world, then I think that's abuse. It's different for everybody. If you can't maintain yourself, if you can't take care of yourself, then you've done too much. It's like binge alcoholics. If you make yourself sick and you're hurting yourself, then I think that's a problem.

Personally, I don't want to abuse something to the point where I can't take care of myself. If I'm no longer sure about what's going on around me or I'm no longer confident to get up and leave the room, that's definitely a problem. Maybe once every couple of months I might smoke some pot, but it just doesn't hold any appeal to me any more, which is really an odd thing for me to say, but it's very cool.

It was the desire to be close to my family that helped me, and their belief in me that I could accomplish what I set out to do. Things now are going well with my family. My sister and I are very close. The first building block to me reestablishing my life was reestablishing my ties with them. My dad and I are very close. I just got done spending a week with him and it's to the point where he can say, "I'm

really proud of you. I'm really proud of what you're doing right now." My mother still has anxiety about what I'm doing. She's not going to be entirely comfortable with my life until I've completed college and have a good nine-to-five job. But they definitely mean a lot to me and I don't want to lose them.

There are days where I have complete confidence in myself and I don't care what other people think. I kind of bounce out of the house and I can take on anything that happens. Probably about once a week I get that happy. I have to learn my life lessons just like everybody else does. It's not as if that was it and now I'm done. Absolutely not. There's still a lot more out there that I need to get over and work through.

When I talk to other young people who might be in a situation like I was, I tell them there has to be something in your life that triggers you to pull out of it. You need to figure out if you're happy. Who are the important people in your life? Who do you look up to? Why are they the way they are, and what is your relationship with them? Is it developing in a good way or are you lying to them? Where do you see yourself in a few years from now? If you can't picture that even, then that itself says something.

Now that I've reached a certain balance with myself and the world around me, I need to figure out what I want to do and take some kind of progressive step towards it. The appeal of school right now for me is to have more options and to be learning new things. I never felt that way about school before. At the same time, I'm not really motivated to go to school and do the extra work that's involved with it. So I'm taking my time and waiting for when I feel it's the right time to do it. I'm aware that it's something that I should do, and that I want to do for myself. Traveling interests me right now. Seeing the world and trying to experience as much of it as I can, trying to fill my life up with as many different positive things as I can, so when it's over I can look back and say, "I took every opportunity I had," and not regret anything, not regret not trying something.

"Just Say No" Doesn't Work

Wind Hughes

The 'Just Say No' approach to confronting drug abuse, adopted in the United States during the Reagan administration, doesn't work, in part, because few young people are going to talk about drug use with someone who judges them severely.

The truth is that many teens will experiment with drugs - from illegal ones (i.e., cocaine) to socially condoned ones (i.e., alcohol) to things we don't even see as drugs (i.e., consumerism). After twenty years of working with adults and teens on the issues of substance use and abuse, I know that kids can tell within minutes if there is safety in speaking to an adult honestly about their experiences, good or bad. I have also found that one of the best ways to prevent drug abuse is for a teen to hear the truth from people who have had experience themselves and who listen in a nonjudgmental manner.

I have met many people of all ages, from a vast variety of backgrounds, who have experimented with drugs in an attempt to alter their state of mind, consciousness, or mood. There was a time in my life when I experimented too, using some drugs and abusing others. It was the sixties and drugs were everywhere. As I grew older, I became aware of more sacred uses of psychedelics; those experiences were life-changing for me. I discovered a deep connection with my spiritual self and, as many say, I saw God within me. These are risky things to say. If you're wanting to hear that *all* drugs under *all* circumstances ruin lives, then stop reading here.

In some cultures - that of the Koryaks in Russia, for example, or the Huichols in Mexico - psychedelics are used as part of sacred religious rituals, with elders to guide those explorations into the deeper self and spirit. These drugs are not used recreationally. In western culture, we have few rituals and guides in place to support our pursuit of inner exploration with or without drugs. Rituals in our consumer culture seem to exist more around shopping, than around what is sacred. We

Nine Facts about Drugs

1) The National Clearing House for Alcohol and Drug Information says that 60 percent of college women who acquired a sexually transmitted disease such as AIDS were under the influence of alcohol at the time they had intercourse.

2) Women become more intoxicated than men when drinking the same amount of alcohol (National Clearing House for Alcohol and Drug Information).

3) More than all other drugs combined, alcohol is associated with domestic violence, assault, homicide, and suicide (National Clearing House for Alcohol and Drug Information).

4) Reflecting a pattern of increased cigarette smoking among women, lung cancer has passed breast cancer as the leading fatal cancer for women (National Clearing House for Alcohol and Drug Information).

5) The National Institute of Drug Abuse rates withdrawal from alcohol as worse than that from heroin. Nicotine falls just below heroin.

6) Even though there is no empirical evidence indicating that marijuana causes permanent brain damage, Dale Gieringer reports in Marijuana Health Mythology that persistent deficits in short-term memory have been noted in chronic, heavy marijuana smokers, even *after* six to twelve weeks of abstinence.

7) Gieringer also reports that research shows the two major risks of excessive marijuana use are

a) Respiratory disease due to smoking;

b) Accidental injuries due to impairment.

8) According to information released in "Pulse Check," a report by the Office of National Drug Control Policy, fewer than 20 percent of people undergoing drug treatment are in treatment for heroin. The majority of people are in treatment for cocaine or alcohol abuse. Marijuana is rarely the primary drug of abuse of people in treatment *except* in programs for juveniles. One third of the people in treatment for marijuana use are under twenty years old.

9) The sign at the U.S./Canadian border states that possession of *any* drug in *any* quantity is considered drug smuggling.

Daughters of the Moon, Sisters of the Sun

seek the five-second fast lane to joy, the instant fix.

Some adults use substances in moderation - a glass of wine at dinner, for example - and describe their experiences as pleasant and life-enriching. Research shows that some drugs enhance certain aspects of brain function such as creativity, abstract thought, and therapeutic self-exploration. Ecstasy, a widely available street drug and favorite of the rave scene, has been used for years as a therapeutic tool in clinical settings, helping people to make positive changes in their lives. Other people use drugs to help them connect with the sacred within themselves.

Our natural state of being, the one we are born with, is an expanded consciousness that contracts as we become identified with our ego, thoughts, and beliefs. When we have powerful, positive experiences on drugs that expand our consciousness, we must remember that these experiences are only the shadow of what is real. How often do we mistake the path for the destination, or the key to the lock for freedom?

Then there's the downside. I've known people who were able to use certain drugs in moderation but who eventually came to abuse them and became so emotionally numb they couldn't feel anything. Some became addicts. And some lost their lives to abuse.

People often ask how you know if you are abusing or addicted. It doesn't matter if the drug is food, sex, consumerism, synthetic, or natural. When you depend upon anything in order to carry out an action (like get over stage fright or perform better in sports) or to feel a certain way, and you can no longer perform those actions or feel those feelings without the substance, you are psychologically addicted. When your body can no longer maintain its equilibrium without a drug, you are physically addicted. If you need it to feel 'high,' you are in trouble. You can be an abuser or addict without using daily, so it is important to look at your relationship with a drug, not just at the frequency of use.

I've worked with users and addicts long enough to be able to say that what is harmful for one person may not be harmful for someone else. But physically addictive substances such as heroin and nicotine are addictive for everyone. There is no way out of this. If you use them, in time you will become addicted. I never knew an addict who started using because he or she wanted to become an addict. Many thought it would never happen to them.

The bottom line is that any form of drug can be dangerous. Many people try drugs without even knowing what their ingredients are, what the proper dosage is, or what the physical and emotional effects will be. Even if you have investigated the effects and chemical properties of a drug, the reality is that what you buy on the street is cut so many times with other, often toxic, chemicals that what you think is pure, good stuff is most often not.

Many of us have done things in our lives because someone else suggested it or pressured us to, or maybe it just looked like a cool thing to do. If you are feeling cool because you are *using*, your sense of knowing who you are has become confused with that feeling of coolness. *You* are not coolness; you are something far deeper and greater than any feeling,

emotion, or substance. When you overdose, you overdose alone. When you get arrested, you go to jail alone, your friends are not there and it is certainly not cool. When you die, you die alone and you don't take coolness with you.

If you're going to use drugs, use them with utmost respect and caution. There is a lot of information on drugs, alcohol, cigarettes, and other substances. Try to find someone who you feel safe with and ask them for help in finding this information, or go to the library and do your own research. There is also a lot of information on how to achieve greater joy and deeper levels of self-exploration and on how to cope with emotional pain and to transform that energy into something productive. Whether you decide to use a substance or not it is a personal decision, one that should be made based on accurate information about its chemistry, its physical and emotional effects, and the personal and legal consequences of its use. This is *your* life, *your* body, *your* choice!

THREE

GROWING UP FAST
AND SPEAKING OUT

~

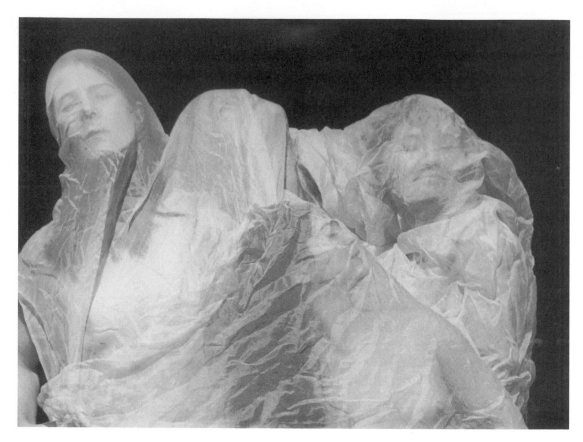

Phoebe Caulfield

I had a dream. I was at the nursing home where my grandfather lay in his casket. I never liked him and I didn't care that he was dead. So I left and went to a nightclub where there was a rave going on.

A bunch of people led me to a back room which was lit with laser lights. There was this guy there who picked up a dead pig and started to rape me with it. He was laughing and having a great time. Then he laid me down in front of him, took a knife and slashed my belly open, and started to rape the wound. Then it was the next day, the day of my grandfather's funeral. I kept going up to everyone and asking them to look at me. I wasn't sure if what I'd experienced was rape or no big deal. I kept going up to people I knew from the past,

Daughters of the Moon, Sisters of the Sun

asking them to look at my scar, but they were watching TV. Finally I went to my mom and said, "Oh, mama, please look at this scar, please look, is there something wrong?" But she didn't seem to care. She kept saying that it would heal. Finally I went back to the funeral and showed it to my dead grandfather. He sat up, looked at it, shook his head, and laid back down. And that was the end of my dream.

I think I was about two-and-a-half or three years old the first time my father molested me, although I don't know if I remember one time in particular or if all the memories are rolled in one. It would start with his saying, "Come sit by me." I remember how my stomach would sink. I would feel sick, but obediently I would go and sit next to him, usually on the couch in the living room. I would sit and he would cover us in this pink-and-green afghan and we would watch TV. I suppose that what actually happened underneath the blanket is not that bad compared to some horror stories I've heard, yet it was enough to affect my behavior with boys later on. He would put his hands on my private parts and sometimes pet, sometimes tickle. I would sit frozen, afraid to move,

afraid to talk.

I remember once looking into the kitchen and watching my stepmother make dinner. I felt angry at her. I couldn't understand why she didn't stop this. It occurs to me now that she probably didn't know what was happening. However, some of that resentment is still there.

You might be asking why I didn't say no. Well, let me tell you something about my father. He is a terrifying man, raised in an alcoholic, military family, beaten and humiliated by my grandfather. He is very short but he seems ten foot tall to me. He hardly ever talks, but he yells. Whenever he was home, I'd always be aware of where he was in the apartment.

When I was in kindergarten, the school counselor came into our classroom. She talked about good touch and bad touch. I knew what my father was doing to me didn't feel good, but when the counselor spoke I knew for sure for the first time that what was happening to me was wrong. I got very excited and made an appointment to talk with her right away, but I wasn't able to tell. Instead, I made up some story about how my parents fought. That was the only time I ever tried to get help.

One afternoon when I was twelve, I was alone in the house and had Oprah on. The show was about molestation. I was washing the dishes and halfway listening until I heard a story that sounded like mine. A rush of memories came back. I remember because I dropped and broke a dish in the sink. I started to cry and cried for a long time.

When I was fourteen, I had my first boyfriend. We went together for two months and went from holding hands to oral sex pretty quick. After we broke up, he still wanted to have sex with me. He was no longer interested in a relationship, just sex. We would do it on the weekends, but during the week he wouldn't talk to me at all. For some reason I kept on going back to him. Then things got worse. He started hitting me. It started as a joke, but then he would hit me for real. One day he smacked me to the floor because I broke his necklace. He was sitting on top of me and hitting me until two of my girlfriends came over by accident and made him stop. But the next day I called him and was just "hey," and by the next night we were back together again. He used to let his friend hold me down and touch me. One time they got handcuffs and they handcuffed me. Once they duct-taped me, but the time they handcuffed me was the worst. I screamed so loud that they had to stop because they were afraid the neighbors would call the police. But I still kept doing stuff with him. I keep going back no matter what he did to me.

That next summer I had sex with four different guys, none of whom I was going out with. I didn't want to, but I couldn't say no. I hated sex, I hated myself, and I hated my life. I never felt so alone, and yet I kept doing it. I hated sex so much that I learned how to shut myself out when it was happening, just like when I was little with my father. That Christmas I slept with five guys in two weeks, two on the same night.

At the end of my senior year, a girl in school confided in me that she was going to a group for people who had survived sexual abuse. When I got home that day, I called the clinic to find out about it. I started going the following week. It's because of that group that I was finally able to tell what happened to me.

At college last year I met a really nice guy. We've been together for five months now and it's been really good. In that time I have learned to enjoy sex, something I never did before. He is the only person outside of this group who knows my story. He is kind to me when I talk to him about what happened, though it is hard for him to listen to it.

It scares me to think that nobody would ever want to marry me. I wouldn't marry anyone just because they wanted to marry me. If I did that, I know I wouldn't be faithful. It's so easy for me to dissociate myself. That's what I did with my dad. I believe marriage is a promise. When I get married, I want to totally want my husband. I want him to be 'the one' and I want to know it for sure. I want to want him every second he's around and be intrigued by everything he says. I don't want to have to look any further than him because he'll be all I need. We'll be like one person. I've seen relationships like that. My aunt and uncle are like that. They rarely fight. They love to be together with each other and do little things for each other. I want to be that happy with someone one day.

I still haven't told my mother about what happened to me. I don't have the guts to tell her. I don't know what would happen to my family if I told. I don't know if we could sur-vive it and I don't want to hurt my dad. I still love him. Really, he is a good person. And he loved me like you wouldn't believe. He adored me. I was his favorite. He thinks everything I do is part of him. Maybe someday I'll be able to confront my dad about what happened, but if I don't, at least I'll have some peace with the fact that I shared my story and maybe that will help somebody else. It's helped me a lot to tell.

The Courage to Heal
Linda Wolf

The night after I listened to Phoebe, I went down to my cabin to sleep. From my loft I looked out my window into a clear sky of twinkling stars. It was so quiet and I thought about how our planet looks so beautiful in the NASA photos from space - watery shades of the most pristine greens and blues - while down here on Earth our human lives are so full of darkness.

I thought about Phoebe's father and the

actions of brutes and bullies who dare to harm children. I thought back to my own teenage years, remembering incident after incident when I allowed myself to be abused because I didn't know I could ask for something better. I didn't think I deserved better. Back then, my experiences never seemed that crucial or important but they have affected and, in many ways, directed every aspect of my relationships with men, in particular my father and husband. These experiences are part of my foundation and, like Phoebe, I didn't really start to heal until I told people who cared.

Now I see that my experiences were typical of the way women and girls are regarded by society. In the United States alone, the FBI estimates that a woman is raped every six minutes. More than half the victims are girls under eighteen. Over 250,000 children, mostly girls, are sexually molested in their homes each year - usually by men in their families. In rural India, many young, newly wedded women are burned to death in what are covered up as 'kitchen fires' but which in truth are dowry burnings - the all-powerful mother-in-law douses her daughter-in-law with cook-

ing oil and sets her on fire. In Africa, women are fighting to stop female genital mutilation - the ceremonial removal of all or part of a girl's labia and clitoris, physically impairing her and depriving her of any sexual pleasure in her lifetime.

As the international women's movement gains strength through forums and grassroots activism, women are uniting and rising up all over the world, demanding to be heard and calling for the abuses to stop. We're forcing people to look at our experience for a change. We're saying, "Look at women's history. See the injustices we live with. We don't want to be stereotyped and we don't want to be dominated by men anymore."

I've heard that in rural villages in the Middle East, families live so close together that when women hear another woman being abused, they come out on their porches and raise a cacophony, banging pots and pans to call attention to it, to stop it and shame the husband, father, uncle, or brother. In the United States, Canada, and Europe we're marching in "Take Back the Night" rallies and drawing attention to the epidemic abuse of women and girls. We are raising our voices and speaking out in myriad ways, through literature, poetry, performance art, and activism. And yes, we are unleashing chaos and changing the way sexual relations are constructed and consequently how they influence society's economic, religious, and political structures and all our personal relationships.

It's clear that women's power is growing and that many men are angry and afraid because of it. Groups like the Promise Keepers have gained hundreds of thousands of followers, mostly male Christian fundamentalists, who believe that women's submissive and subservient roles are *ordained* by God and who can prove it using biblical quotes. In her book *Backlash: The Undeclared War Against American Women*, Susan Faludi argues that the backlash serves to pressure women back into their 'acceptable' roles as daddy's-little-girls or 'good housewives.' Some people insist that if women got the power, we'd just use it to turn the tables on men. But what most women want is equality, partnership, and balance, not matriarchy replacing patriarchy.

So many boys and men are realizing how hurt they, too, have been by the stereotypes of their gender. Many say they are ashamed of being men because of what men have done to women and girls. We won't get anywhere by having them feel guilty. We need to be equal partners. As Riane Eisler says in her book *Sacred Pleasure: Sex, Myth, and the Politics of the Body,* we live in a time when "man's conquest of nature" threatens all life on our planet. We must look at things from a partnership, instead of a dominator, way of thinking in *all* our relationships - social, political, economic, and spiritual. It's going to take each of us, women and men together, to work it out. We can't blame each other or the boys and men today for the unjust actions of yesterday. We can only ask them to stand with us to change the way it is, not just between men and women, but for all oppressed peoples. And we must come to the understanding that sexual relations are about conscious, equal connections, the erotic being sacred, and our bodies being shrines. Then we can get on to healing the earth and making *this* the true garden of Eden.

Linda Wolf talks with
Maya Angelou

*D*r. Maya Angelou, author and professor of American studies at Wake Forest University, has been hailed as one of the great voices of contemporary literature.*

Linda: There's a girl in one of our groups who was molested by her father when she was young. She's never told anyone, even her mother, and he is not hurting her now. She says that even though he is a small man and that what happened to her was a mild thing, she is still afraid of him.

Dr. Angelou: No, no, those are two mistakes.

* *Portions of this interview originally appeared in* In Context *magazine, Issue #43.*

There is no 'mild molestation' and no brute is ever small. The man or woman who is brutalizing somebody could be four foot tall, but the molester is never small and no molestation is ever mild. It attacks the very spirit. I can only say to her, "I feel with you," because once one is molested it's very hard to feel clean again. Very hard. I spent almost seven years not talking [after being raped]. So tell her you feel with her - not *for* her or *to* her but *with* her. And I would encourage her to get counseling as soon as possible.

Linda: After all you've been through, including being raped as a child, how did you continue to have good feelings for yourself, to like yourself?

Dr. Angelou: I don't know if I continue, even today, always liking myself. But what I learned to do many years ago was to forgive myself. It is very important for every human being to forgive herself or himself because if you live, you will make mistakes - it is inevitable. But once you do and you see the mistake, then you forgive yourself and say, "Well, if I'd known better I'd have done better," that's all. So you say to people you think you may have injured, "I'm sorry," and then you say to your-

self, "I'm sorry." If we hold on to the mistake, we can't see our own glory in the mirror because we have the mistake between our faces and the mirror; we can't see what we're capable of being. You can ask forgiveness of others, but in the end the real forgiveness is in one's own self. I think that young men and women are so caught by the way they see themselves. Now mind you, when a larger society sees them as unattractive, as threats, as too black or too white or too poor or too fat or too thick or too sexual or too asexual, that's rough. But you can overcome that. The real difficulty is to overcome how you think about yourself. If we don't have that we never grow, we never learn, and sure as hell we should never teach.

Linda: You've done a lot of things in your life that most people would judge as wrong. You've smoked pot, taken drugs, you were a madam for lesbian prostitutes, a teenage mom, a table dancer - you didn't follow the straight and narrow. All these experiences gave you a rich life?

Dr. Angelou: Yes, but I wouldn't suggest it for anybody. I mean, if you happen to fall into that sort of experience, what you have to do is forgive yourself. If you're in the very gutter, see where you are and admit it. As soon as you admit it, you can be like the prodigal son, the prodigal daughter. Get up and go home - wherever home is. Get up and go to a safe place, someplace where your spirit is not kicked and brutalized and your body not misused and abused. Get up. But you can't get up unless you see where you are and admit it.

I wrote about my experiences because I thought too many people tell young folks, "I never did anything wrong. Who, *moi?* - never I. I have no skeletons in my closet. In fact, I have no closet." They lie like that and then young people find themselves in situations and they think, "Damn I must be a pretty bad guy. My mom or dad never did anything wrong." They can't forgive themselves and go on with their lives. So I wrote the book *Gather Together in My Name.* Meaning that all those grown people, all those adults, all those parents and grandparents and teachers and preachers and rabbis and priests who lie to the children can gather together in my name and I will tell them the truth. Wherever you are, you have got to admit it and set about to make a change. That's why I wrote that book.

It's the most painful book I've ever written.

Linda: Do you see hope for this world?

Dr. Angelou: Oh, yes

Linda: What do you tell young people who see nothing but the world falling apart?

Dr. Angelou: It seems terrible. There's racism and sexism and ageism and all sorts of idiocies. But bad news is not news. We've had bad news as a species for a long time. We've had slavery and human sacrifice and the holocaust and brutalities of such measure. We can't imagine what Attila the Hun did or the cruelties of the period when the church, the great Inquisition, sliced people open from their heads to their groin and gutted them. And women were burned at the stake and stoned to death, as were men. We can't imagine it. Today we say, "Ah, how horrible." But the truth is, we have had bad news a long time. Yet, amazingly, we have survived. And while on the one hand we have the brutes, the bigots, and the bullies, at the same time we have had men and women who dreamed great dreams. We've had Galileo and Aesop, Paul Laurence Dunbar and W.E.B. DuBois. We've had Sholem Asch, and Shalom Aleichem - great dreamers. We've had women who stood alone, whether it was Harriet Tubman or Mother Jones. We've had Margaret Sanger. We've had women who have stood in the gap and said, "I'm here to try to save the world."

You have to think who we are. If you made a map five miles long and five miles wide of the universe, Earth would be smaller than a pin-head. I think it may have been Durant who said if you make a model the size of the Empire State Building, and flat on the top of the spire you put a postage stamp, the model would represent how long Earth has been here, the spire would represent how long life has been here, the thickness of the stamp would represent how long human beings have been here, and the thickness of the ink would represent how long we've been sentient. So we're the newest group on this little blob of spit and sand.

This is what young women and men should know. They should know that we are carnivorous, yet we have decided somehow not only not to eat our brothers and sisters, who may be delicious, but to accord them some rights and to try to love them and look after them. I don't want young men and women looking around and saying, "Oh my God, oh mea culpa, it's so awful." It's bad but it's also good, and it's up to each one of us to make it better. Every one of us. We deserve our future.

Linda: What advice do you have for girls?

Dr. Angelou: To laugh as much as possible, always laugh. It is the sweetest thing one can do for oneself and one's fellow human being. When people see the laughing face, even if they're jealous of it, their burden is lightened. But do it first for yourself. Laugh and dare to try to love somebody, starting with yourself.

Linda: It's hard to love.

Dr. Angelou: It's hard because people think they have something to lose and the truth is they have everything to gain in trying to love somebody. You must love yourself first, of course, and you must protect yourself when you can. Protect yourself so that nobody over-rides you, overrules you, or steps on you. You say, "Just a minute, I'm worth everything, dear." If you really realize that, you realize everybody else is worth everything. Everybody. Fat and thin and plain and pretty, white and black and rich and poor, thick and slow and brilliant. Everybody is worth everything. Start with yourself, though.

Sarah Lindsley

I was born in Hawaii but we moved to San Diego when my real dad got sick. He died before Christmas, when I was four. My mom met Don when I was seven and they married when I was almost nine, so he was my father for the next six years.

Daughters of the Moon, Sisters of the Sun

I always called him Don and not Dad, mostly because I couldn't get used to the sound of the word 'Dad' coming off of my lips. I still have a hard time when I'm talking about my first father. I don't know what to call him. Daddy? It sounds really strange for me to call anyone that.

I don't remember ever thinking about there being any other option but 'straight' till about fifth grade, when 'dyke' became an insult. My best friend was Lindsay and she got called 'Lezy Lindsay' and I remember her crying like it was the worst insult. I thought that gay people were weird. I didn't think of them as anyone I would know, or myself, God forbid. I had this horrible stereotype. I don't know where I picked it up, but I imagined that if I met a lesbian, she'd be like a man, really ugly and coarse and just gross. So I met this bisexual man. I didn't know him. He was a friend of my karate teacher. I remember thinking, "Is my karate teacher gay? That can't be, because he's a cool guy." So I figured he wasn't gay. I remember having crushes on girls at this time. I read in a book somewhere that everyone has a homosexual experience at some point. So I thought, "Okay, I'm still cool."

There was this girl named Lisa who I had a crush on for a while, so I felt that was my homosexual experience. It was a normal stage. I'd get over it at some point and it would all be cool, but I was definitely not gay.

I was very attracted to guys. My friend Lindsay and I were like the raging hormone sisters. We'd talk about guys all of the time: guys, guys, guys. Though going out with guys was more like a social thing. It was mostly just holding hands. I didn't kiss a guy until ninth grade. That was really late. Most of the people I knew were kissing guys. I'd go out with a guy for a week. We'd talk on the phone, go to a movie or something, and hold hands. That would be it.

Then in ninth grade my dad (Don) got sick. It was the craziest year of my life. He had pancreatic cancer. It had already progressed to the liver by the time we knew what it was. There was not much hope, but we hoped anyway. I started spending a lot of time away from home. He was on morphine all of the time because he was in so much pain. He'd be hallucinating and wouldn't know who I was. I didn't want to be around that.

That's when I started doing theater. It

was a place where I could spend a lot of time, being someone else and not be where and who I really was. I started hanging out with this group from school. I met my first boyfriend, Max. I started dating him and going out every weekend, for the whole weekend, with him and his friends. I was at Max's house when my dad died. I was watching a movie: *Yellow Submarine.* Max was my first sexual partner and I had my first orgasm with him. I actually started being sexual the day my dad died. It was really odd that it happened that way. I continued being sexual with Max after that. I dated nonstop. I didn't really stop dating until this year.

In California I started going to the Unitarian Church. I had tried to become Christian way back when. I was really Christian, like by the book, and I went to a Baptist Church for a long time. I guess it was my way of rebelling because my parents were so *not* - Christian. When my dad got sick, I got angry at God for doing this to me. Then I started to realize that it was all bullshit. So there was this Unitarian Church. I thought it was a cool place. They're not dogmatic and they're really free and I liked that. I started going to the youth group

where there were tons of gay people, maybe fifty percent gay. This was the first time I was ever around gay people. And I thought, "They are like normal people." It was then that I started to become aware of myself sexually and more aware of my attraction to girls. For the first time, I considered homosexuality as an option.

I had crushes on girls over the years. I felt, "This is a girl I like and admire," not "This is a girl I'm interested in." I never thought of it as a gay crush. I was thinking to myself, as I was meeting these people who were gay, that it might be a possibility for me. But at the same time I was dating Max and getting more sexual with him. So I had this conversation with Lindsay and I don't remember if I brought it up or she did, but we talked and talked and talked. It was the first time I verbally stated that I might be gay. She thought maybe she was gay too. The next day she said to me, "I decided I'm not gay." So I said, "Me too," even though I'd sort of been thinking I might be. I said no because she said she wasn't and I didn't want to admit that I *might* be because she was my best friend and we'd been doing everything the same since fifth grade.

I decided that I was pretty sure I was bi, but I didn't tell anyone about it till I went to this gay rights march with my church. It was so awesome. I still have the poster that I carried on my wall. It says, "Love Sees No Gender." Everyone was saying "Gay is good." It was wonderful! It was so uplifting and positive. So right after that I told my friends I was gay. They said, "Oh really? Cool." No big deal. Why didn't I tell them this before? We had all come from the junior high experience of being anti-gay, and we were now going to this church and seeing that gays were cool people. I'm glad that they had gone through that exposure with me, otherwise I think it would have made coming out a lot harder. I still didn't tell my mom or any of my family then. Things became easier and I felt freer to feel my feelings. At that point it wasn't an option for me to flirt with girls because I was still dating guys. Though I had a crush on Eddie Sloughton's sister most of the time that I was dating him. That was really odd.

I didn't have any idea how to go about acting on my feelings about girls. At that point I didn't have any fantasies about girls that were very extensive, beyond kissing. I was

fifteen and I had this friend and we were both newly bisexual and we hadn't had any experience, but we both wanted to see what it was all about. It was interesting. We had fun though we only did it that one night.

I consider myself bisexual in that I could have sexual relations with a guy or a girl. But I'm turned off at the idea of doing anything with a penis. I just don't want a penis near me. I guess I could do something above the waist with a guy, but that may just be a phase I'm going through. When it comes to guys, it's been disappointing. It wasn't like I did something I didn't want to do. Not like I couldn't say no. I never had that problem. It was more that I was never really satisfied. I liked the kissing and I liked the closeness, but the sexual aspect of it got worse and worse. I didn't even care. We'd be having sex and I'd think, "I hope this is over so that I can cuddle."

It was exciting with women. Everything was new and I felt like everything was more equal, there was a give and take. When I was with a guy I felt like *he* was having a good time but I was waiting for what was coming afterwards. And when it comes to orgasm, it took a lot for me to have an orgasm with a guy. I came to orgasm more easily with women. With a girl I can have an orgasm without even going down, with just kissing and fooling around. It just happens. It's never been that way with a guy.

spent a lot of time not wanting to be with anyone else. Last spring I had a relationship with this guy named Ty. I don't know why I did it. Looking back, I think I was trying to see if I still could have a relationship with a guy that

It's hard for me to say where I'm at now because I haven't had a sexual relationship in a long time. There was this girl I was interested in very much for a year and a half, but she was straight. She was my best friend and I

was rewarding. And it wasn't. I went into that wanting to be worshipped in a way. I wanted someone to look at my body and say, "Wow, that's attractive." I wanted it, but when I got it I didn't want it anymore. That's the only sexual relationship I've had since I've been experimenting with girls.

I have a lot of anger towards the world, both for its sexism and its homophobia. I guess my awareness around women's issues has changed a lot of my attitudes. I see most guys - I'm making a generalization here - as not having a clue about what women go through. I find it hard to reach guys on that level. Even the ones that are really trying to understand - they just can't. They definitely can't understand my anger. When I'm talking to guys, girls too, I find myself trying to censor what I feel, especially when it comes to anger, because I don't want to be branded a feminazi or a man hater. I don't hate men but I have a lot of anger towards the things that men do to women.

I get angry when I look at the role models that women have and I read the magazines and I look at what women are presented to be. What can I be if I'm a woman? I can be an actress and have my body exploited. I mean, that's what actresses are now. They're bodies, they're faces. Or I could be somebody's mother and be a nice woman and have no sexuality. Especially in the movies, all of the intelligent women are also bodies. They come in to be the expert and they fall in love with the man and that's their role. It seems like people recognize this and at the same time they don't. It seems like people are so blind.

The most recent thing that's made me angry was this article I read in *Vanity Fair,* on Uma Thurman. I really like Uma Thurman and I think she's an incredibly talented actress. They called her "disturbingly beautiful." What made me mad is the way they had the pictures juxtaposed to the words. It had this picture of her lounging in lingerie, and right next to this was this paragraph that said how she had stopped doing movies for a while because she found she was being represented as a body and she wanted to be more than that. I couldn't figure out why she did this article. It says in large print above the article "Marriage was a mistake." Thank god she's divorced now so that we can have the body back. Like, she couldn't be a sexual being if she was married. They said, "She's surprisingly smart," like "She has a brain, aren't you surprised?" It made me so mad. And this is a women's magazine.

Sometimes I feel that no one understands what I'm saying. I guess I'm struggling to make myself heard. I don't want to say any-thing too controversial. Not because I'm afraid but because I want people to hear me. I want to say it in such a way that people won't blow me off. And I don't know how to do that.

I feel very lucky. My mom has become very accepting and I've always had friends that are really accepting. I've been able to be fairly open about my sexuality here in the focus group, and I've never been attacked, verbally or physically. Still, it can be hard. It's hard to be surrounded by straight people in a straight world, especially in a smaller town. I want to tell girls that you may feel like you are alone, but it's important to know that you are not alone out there. Even if you are in a place that's not accepting, you're not stuck there. You can find a place that is accepting. And it is not a bad thing to be gay. In fact, it is awesome. I wouldn't change it if I could.

As for the future, I see myself with a woman as a partner, having children, a family, and lots of dogs. But I don't know, that could change. I'm still struggling with the idea of artificial insemination. I think it's a little bit weird. But I want to have kids and I want to be with a woman. I really want to be pregnant and give birth. You never know. I could fall in love with a guy.

I worry about having kids if I'm a parent in a homosexual relationship. It's totally not accepted. It's one thing to be gay and it's another thing to be gay and have kids. That's the whole thing the Christian coalition is bat-tling in the United States. On the college appli-cations I was filling out it asked for father and mother. Not parents. I'm more concerned about the social implications of being gay. More for the child's sake than my own. I'm okay. I feel like I can face the world. It's hard for a kid growing up. Any way you're different is a major thing and I don't know if that's going to change before I have kids. I doubt that it's going to change that radically.

Right now I call myself a lesbian bisexu-al. I heard that phrase and thought, "Oh sure, that's me." I'm a bisexual who's decided to be with women. So that's where I am.

McKenzie Nielsen

The summer I turned six, I was sexually molested by my next-door neighbor. It made me sick and numb. I felt betrayed by him as an adult who should have taken care of me. This launched me into a sexual awareness I wouldn't have discovered on my own until much later.

One day I told my mother. She asked me why I didn't tell her sooner and I said, "I just didn't think that you could do anything about it." My parents didn't put me on trial, wanting to protect me and thinking it would get better over time. The child molester got therapy and I was told not to talk about it. But even though the molestation stopped, I had become aware of my body and sexual feelings. I had never imagined people did things like that, and I began to explore my body, innocently thinking I was the only girl who felt a dark, warm feeling when I touched myself or let the bath water cascade over my clitoris. This experience belonged to no one else; it was all mine. I guarded it, and still do.

When I was ten I made a best friend who shared my taste for the erotic. We sneaked *Playgirl* from her older sister and secretly watched *9 1/2 Weeks*. These things didn't seem real to me; what I liked was to watch her masturbate. Sometimes we would use the vibrator, one of those 'foot massagers' her mom had lying around, trading off, never touching each other. Other times, and these were my favorite, we would take long bubble baths together, exploring orgasms using the

pressure of the tap water. When she moved away a few years later, I returned to the status of lone masturbator, missing her and knowing it would be a long time before intimacy would be that easy again. Eventually I entered the dating scene at school, kissing guy after guy like it was my mission. I kissed them all but I hated it. My conclusion was that love and sex must make kissing worth it. I wanted to experiment with both as soon as possible. Love was a big thing to me, the ultimate goal of life as far as I was concerned, but reserved for 'the one.' Love is the thing that is sacred.

When I was fourteen, I fell for a boy much older than me. This was the first time I knew what it was to crave another person's body, to want to possess, taste, and tease their skin to desire. The fact that I couldn't have him made him more delicious. We became friends and I spent every moment trying to turn our friendship into a relationship. When I was fifteen, I slept with him. We didn't plan it. We didn't use a condom. I never said no; he never asked. I knew he didn't feel as strongly for me as I did for him, but I was convinced that he could grow to love me or I could change myself into something that he could love.

The sex was awful, rushed, and incomplete. I was disappointed, but I loved him and it seemed an honor to me to fulfill his momentary sexual needs. The next week he told me that there were no feelings on his part, that this was an accident, that he had been drunk. I had the sudden urge to hurt him so badly. I wanted to castrate him so he would never be able to make that mistake again. Instead I took the blow, determined to keep him close to me no matter how much it hurt. My silence at that moment, my strength or stupidity, has contributed to so much confusion for both of us.

For me, sex with men creates a distance between us instead of bringing us together. Because of the way men are. Because they rarely think about what a woman wants. I feel badly saying this because I do like some of the men I've been with, but it's just that I feel used when it's over, when they're done with me. I let myself be used because accommodating to their needs is easier than trying to get mine met. I would want to please them because it's fun to make somebody feel good, but it wasn't mutual. They didn't try to please me. Even if they tried, they'd be doing it in a selfish way, as if our orgasms are theirs, like some trophy, proof of their manhood. For this reason, even though I slept with many of them, I never once had an orgasm or even came close. I know that this happens to many women. It's a tragedy. But for me it's not the orgasms I felt lacking in sex; it was the intimacy and I feel that is where men fail. It's our society's fault. It teaches men to distance themselves from their feelings. So, of course, they can't go there with another person; they can't even go there with themselves. There are some men who have had the courage to step out of this stereotype, but they are few and far between.

When I was in high school, I felt attractions towards women but I felt like I had to keep them to myself. At times I wondered if these feelings were because of my experiences with men, but I realized it wasn't about running away from men but running towards women. Moving to Seattle and starting college gave me the freedom to explore.

My first relationship came out of a close friendship. It was tentative and childlike, completely new to both of us and very improvisational. Even though we never really made love

and we were hesitant about our feelings and identities, it was the most satisfying relationship I had ever experienced. I felt loved and listened to for the first time, opened up and seen as I really am. It lasted only for a summer - we wanted different things - but I will be grateful to her forever for being my first companion in discovery. After this I dated casually, but I always felt like I was the driven lesbian seducing the curious heterosexual. What I wanted was to have my passionate feelings returned as well as my loving feelings. I didn't want there to be gender roles, but I was constantly falling into either 'femme' or 'dyke.' I'm neither, like most lesbians, but people will name you to keep you caged.

It was hard coming out to my parents. I knew they were going to be upset. Especially my mom, who has problems with homosexuality. The thing I was most afraid of was that they would take offense and think that I was

doing it to be different. I love my parents and I never want to hurt them. I waited for a year after I knew for sure it wasn't going to change.

I told my mom first. She was not happy about it. She was afraid of my father's reaction and of the world's response. She was afraid I wouldn't be hired if anyone knew. She tried hard to understand why I would make this choice, but couldn't. It's still really hard for her. I want my parents to be proud of me, but I have to be myself. I have to be open. I want them to know my girlfriends and to be a part of my life. I didn't want them to be distanced from me. They deserve to know that this is my life choice. There are no absolutes, but this is not going to change as far as I can tell.

Currently, I am in a committed relationship with an amazing woman. We have had hard times but we are determined to grow together, to become more ourselves, to be intimate, to share our lives. The truth is, all relationships are difficult, you have to work with them. I think this is the hardest thing for me to learn. As Jeanette Winterson says in her book *Written on The Body*, "I don't know if this is a happy ending but here we are let loose in open fields."

Sarah Lindsley and McKenzie Nielsen talk with the Indigo Girls

*A*my Ray and Emily Saliers, the Indigo Girls, have won a Grammy Award for best contemporary folk album (and have been nominated for Grammys four other times). The duo has sold over six million records and has performed in sixty-one benefit concerts.

Sarah: I was wondering about your personal spirituality and how it relates to your life, your music, and your social activism.

Emily: My dad's a Methodist minister and a professor of theology, so I grew up going to church with my family and being around the sacred language from the Western Christian tradition. In my music, biblical references come naturally, the language of the Bible being so rich in and of itself with great stories and interesting characters. But beyond that,

there is a spirituality underlying some of our music that has nothing to do with specific texts; it's more about how we feel about the world. Personally, I believe in God, I believe in a creator, and I believe that the teachings of Jesus were incredibly beautiful and powerful and I try to follow them in my life. But I don't believe that Christianity is the one and only truth. And I'm not doing activist events for God, so to speak.

Amy: For me, every moment is sacred. I believe in respect for all beings, and my songs are extensions of that. Most of the activism

I'm involved in deals with social justice or environmental issues, sexism, homophobia, religious intolerance, racism. It's all linked - just like the way we treat the environment is a reflection of how we treat women and vice versa.

McKenzie: Do you think as women you've been discriminated against in the music industry?

Emily: We hear about some homophobia going on - people who don't want to play our records because we're gay or they don't like our politics.

Amy: I think discrimination against women is rampant and insidious. MTV discriminates, radio discriminates, the media discriminate, but we're not playing their game so it doesn't affect us that much. We hear about radio programmers who say, "We're already playing three women bands; we can't play another one." We're like, "Oh, well, okay, how many guys are you playing?" But with MTV it's the tits and ass thing. They'll show a few women that don't fit into that, but not many. People say, "Women are getting further than they've ever gotten before in this business," and that's probably true, but on what terms? By what

they're wearing, what their body looks like, what their hair looks like? There's always a token strong woman that you can point to who's doing okay, who's accepted on her own terms, but it's always a fluke.

Linda: When did you discover you were gay and how did you tell the people who mean the most to you?

Emily: The really strange thing is, just before I started to discover that I might be gay, I was very homophobic. I didn't know what it was, so I didn't know how to react. By the time I was nineteen or twenty and I realized I was gay, I was okay with it. But I kept it from my parents for two years. I told my sisters, one by one; it was no big deal. I don't know why I didn't tell my parents. I guess it's because I've always felt really close to my family, and I was afraid I was going to rock the boat in what was pretty much an idyllic family situation. I was afraid I was going to become the black sheep of the family, so I was scared. But then I started thinking about it and I realized that they wouldn't react that way, so I had separate meetings with each of them and I cried, it was very emotional, and they were very accepting. The only thing they were concerned about was would I be well taken care of in terms of love and life. From then on I've always been openly gay in my private life, but it took me a while to get used to the thought of being gay for the press.

Amy: My mom approached me about it. She said there were rumors, she couldn't say the word, we didn't really have a language for it. I said, "Well, I'm in love and I don't know what that means and I haven't been physical yet." I had had a boyfriend, but I was just a senior in high school. So my parents knew and my sisters sort of knew, but there wasn't an open dialogue about it. But when I had my second relationship, it was like, "Okay, there's going to be a dialogue about this because you're my family and it's important to me and we have to learn to talk to each other." Besides, I felt stronger about it myself. I felt clearer because I always liked guys a lot and I wanted to be able to have access to men, too. I don't feel the same pull with them. I want to, but I don't - it's a drag because I like guys a lot.

Wind: You seem to feel free to write about anything in your music.

Emily: Yeah, Amy and I both feel completely free to write about whatever we want to write about or to pick up an instrument we're not good at and play it anyway or to make exactly the kind of record we want to make or wear the clothes we want to wear, and if we're not hip or we're not feminine or whatever it is, then so what? I don't think any human being is truly free. We're so tethered to our insecurities and hampered by our fears and our prejudices. I think it's human nature that we're never going to be free.

Sarah: What do you personally struggle with that keeps you from being free?

Emily: More or less what goes on for a lot of other people - my insecurities, my self-worth. I go through those basic human struggles. This is a very alienating world and you have to be strong and remind yourself that you're okay. We're flooded with commercialism and advertisements that tell us what's cool and what we have to have and what we should be like; there's a lot of cultural homogeneity. So if you're a little off the beaten path, you have to remind yourself that it's a good thing and celebrate the diversity. I'm never totally satisfied with where I am. I'd like to always be better or smarter. If we didn't have that, we'd never grow.

Linda: Do either of you want to be mothers?

Emily: No, but I could get the hormonal surge and want to tomorrow!

Amy: I've wanted to, but I think I want to finish this tour first and then think about it. I really wanted to have kids but I also had a relationship that just ended that was like a seven-year marriage, and I don't want to have kids in the context of being by myself. I think being a mother would be a great experience.

Wind: How do you manage doing all you're doing right now, having just ended a long-term relationship?

Amy: It's been hard, very hard. I'm on the road and I'm going to places that I've shared with somebody I was with and that's rough. But I've gone through so many good things in the last years and I feel like there's a mystery to it all. And while it's painful sometimes, compared to the pain that I've seen other people suffering, it's hard to give myself space to feel that. On another level, I realize that everything's always going to be okay for me. I know where my next meal and my shelter are coming from, and love is an issue that works its way out in one way or another.

McKenzie: Are you afraid of being alone? Are you lonely now that you're broken up?

Amy: No, I think we're all lonely. I think that's the human condition. I think we all feel loneliness, but I'm not afraid of it and I'm not afraid of being alone. I see the suffering of feeling lonely. I have felt loneliness; I've felt lonely with people and without them. But I've only grown from it, learned from it. The negative impact has disappeared for me in the face of all the positive things I've learned. I find that when you get upset by loneliness or you feel like crying or you feel that painful feeling, it isn't a bad thing. I just look at it as feelings. It's like when I read William Faulkner, with all the perversity and the darkness; it's so sad and painful but it's so beautiful as well, and that's how I see loneliness. Out of that arrive all our needs for religion and everything we do. I think if God is a single entity, God is lonely, too, and sometimes I think that's the place we connect.

McKenzie: If you could go back and talk to yourself before you started playing music, what would you tell yourself.

Amy: I would tell myself to practice...

Emily: I'd say that, too. It's funny, the older you get, the more philosophical you might become about life. I feel myself much more at ease about the way things turn and twist. Sometimes I can be a very controlling person in my own life, but the older I get and the more I've settled into my life and career, I just know that things are happening for a reason and that everything is in its place in the shifting of things. So if I could have told myself that, maybe I'd have avoided some anxiety in my life.

McKenzie: Is there a specific message you want people to get from your music?

Amy: I think that we try to talk about respect for each other, the world around us, your self, and the sacredness of life. Especially for women, the self-esteem issue is so relevant all of our lives. We're so free when we start out, and then all of a sudden we get in school and everybody feels like shit. Why is that happening? Emily and I are like, "Get through that and be yourself and respect everything and everyone and know you are good."

Emily: Life is a struggle but there's hope and beauty in the world. Even though a lot of our songs are dark, there's oftentimes the strain of "But we're so powerful as individuals and we're loved and we're good and the things we struggle with are the things that teach us the most and help us to grow." In the end, that's what matters.

The Temple of the Holy Prostitute

Wind Hughes

There was a time in history when our sexuality was not separate from our spirituality, when sex was considered something sacred: a path of purification and unification with God.

It's very different from the way our culture relates to sexuality today: something only for procreation and bodily pleasure.

Many cultures cultivated, and some still do, the art of sex for sensual pleasure and spiritual practice. In ancient Greece, Egypt, and other areas there existed temples called Temples of the Holy Prostitute. In those days, prostitutes were women of high spiritual stature. In these communities, the women took turns in service at these temples. Women and sex were both held as divine, and it was believed that men could reestablish their connection to the divine within them through union with a woman's body. After wars, men would visit the temples to purge and cleanse their souls.

The Gnostics, a group of early Christians who claimed to have received many of their teachings directly from Christ, incorporated similar practices. They believed that through regular sexual union with females, the 'chosen vessels,' one could be united with the light or spark of the divine. (One well-known Gnostic was Valentinus. This may give you a new, more sacred appreciation of Valentine's day.)

Eastern religions hold this same belief in their sacred texts. The Hindus teach Tantra yoga: the yoga of sex. They see sex as the cosmic union of opposites; by practicing techniques designed to awaken what they term the *kundalini* energy in us, this energy is moved up the spine, the polarity of male-female energies is transcended, and God realization is experienced. The Buddhist teachings in the Kama Sutra are based on the same principles. This is why sexual practices are so often depicted in eastern and Asian art.

In her book *Sacred Pleasure*, Riane Eisler says, "It is highly probable that people who inhabited Europe many thousands of years ago celebrated the cyclical return of life, each year at the beginning of spring, through religious rites in which the sexual union of female and male principles was a form of sacrament."

In the book *To Be a Woman*, Deena Metzger speaks about why things changed. She writes, "It is no wonder that from the beginning the first patriarchs, the priests of Judea and Israel, the prophets of Jehovah, all condemned the Holy Prostitutes.... If the priests wished to insert themselves between the people and the divine, they had to remove women from that role. So it was not that sexuality was originally considered sinful per se, or that women's sexuality threatened property or progeny; it was that in order for the priests to have power, women had to be replaced as a road to the divine — this gate had to be closed. It was, we can speculate, to this end that the terrible misogyny we all suffer was instituted." We have learned to be ashamed of something that was once known to be a link to the divine.

In our culture sexuality, especially women's sexuality, has become something to control, avoid, and be ashamed of unless it is being represented as a marketing tool. In advertising, sexuality is glorified not because it's pleasurable or sacred, but because possessing a beautiful, sexy woman has become a symbol of a man's success. Success is associated with having many things and sex sells *things.* It's interesting to me that our culture supports sex as a means of generating large corporate profits, but as soon as a woman chooses to directly profit herself - for instance, by prostitution - it becomes illegal.

With all of the western religious pressure to avoid sex, and because sex is seen as something that takes you *away* from God rather than *to* her, women are confused about their sexuality and have internalized this shame and conflict. We see this confusion internalized as a split of the psyche, projected in the Madonna/whore dichotomy. A woman is a whore if she is openly sexual, especially if she has more than one partner. She's a saint, a Madonna, if she doesn't have sex. We have been taught to disown a most integral aspect of our being, and when it arises in us as a

natural desire or urge, we are told it's 'bad.' No wonder I've found, over my years as a therapist, that so many male clients become uncomfortable with their wife's sexuality once she becomes a mother.

Young women of this generation are struggling to decide whether to be sexual or not. I often ask my female clients to find their connection with their own sexuality - not the sex they have with their partners, but the place in them that holds this sexual energy. Many of them look at me blankly and have no idea what I am talking about. The men I ask rarely have a problem with this concept. They have never had to split off from their own inner sexual being.

We can experience our own sexual energy as something that is ours and does not belong to any other person or any market. It is possible to reclaim our bodies and our sexuality as something inherently sacred and as a direct link to the divine. I believe it is essential to our own healing as women and to the healing of the planet that we do so.

Valerie Fox

My name is Valerie Fox. I was born a Pisces on February 27, 1975. Life has never been easy for me, or even relatively easy. It has all been one great struggle after another.

The Early Years

My parents divorced when I was five. I barely remember living with my mother after the divorce. She was always leaving my brother and me with babysitters. One memory in particular is of her waking us up in the middle of the night, telling me to put our clothing in a paper bag because my brother and I were leaving. I think this is when we went to live with my father.

Living with my father was definitely better. He was there for us almost all of the time except when he was working. Shortly after we moved in, I was sexually molested by a male babysitter. At the time I wasn't aware of how deeply traumatized I was. A year later, a man who was living with us showed me pictures of child pornography. This too had a profound effect on me. My boundaries and sense of self were completely messed up, not to be restored for years.

By the time I was a freshman, I was partying like crazy. I'd slept with over twenty guys and was considered a tramp by the town I lived in. My father didn't realize I was having problems, but thankfully my mother did and she asked me to live with her. I was very

depressed and voluntarily entered a psychiatric hospital and was put on Prozac. After about four weeks I realized I didn't want to be dependent on a drug to deal with my emotions. I wanted to be who I was, feel what was going on, and work with it accordingly. I couldn't do that if the symptoms were being masked. I wanted everything out in the open. Looking back on it all, this was the smartest decision I had ever made. Life has been much better since then.

We moved to Washington and I started my sophomore year at Bainbridge High School, where I met Michael. I had the biggest crush on him but didn't do anything about it until my senior year, at which point I asked him out. We've been together, for the most part, ever since.

Summer 1994

I am nineteen and I've just been arrested for giving LSD to a friend who ended up overdosing. I never realized that my life would completely change over something like this. Having been unofficially charged with two counts of delivery of a controlled substance and one count of possession, all felonies, and after a weekend in jail, I am much wiser. I don't know when I will be arraigned, which makes it difficult to plan a life since I may have to spend up to two years in jail.

My life has been nothing but one big saga. I've always had a longing to have a normal life, to get the attention I need and not have to grow up so fast. I have tried to get that attention from anywhere and anyone I could, and when I didn't get it I didn't know what to do. I ended up causing a lot of problems for myself, for which I take full responsibility. I haven't used much common sense. I always say that things will get better, yet each time it turns out to be the same cycle. I wish that I could be cleansed and truly start anew.

Winter 1995

For the past year and a half I've been in Oregon, going to college and traveling with Michael. We were in Colorado when the call came to go home and face the prosecution for my drug charges. We had been looking at our futures and we decided that it was finally time to go our separate ways. I needed to get out on my own, and we needed to be independent of each other and grow up. Two days later I discovered I was pregnant. I'm not going to have an abortion. We've talked about it and

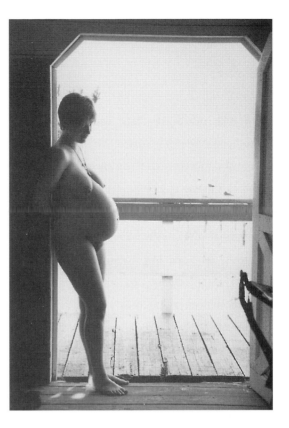

we're committed to going through the pregnancy together and have an open adoption.

I cannot afford to keep a child, and being single parents would be hard. I don't know if we'll be together for the rest of our lives. We want to make sure this child has a family. I always figured I'd be with Michael, having a baby in twenty years, but not now. If we got married now, it would be a forced marriage. I don't even have a life for me yet; I'm staying at my mom's. I don't want to be a stereotypical welfare mother.

Open adoption means we can be part of

the baby's life and the baby will grow up in a home where the people are really prepared for parenting and really want a child. It's a gift for everyone all the way around. I know it will be painful, but that's part of it. How it goes depends upon the people involved. It can be anything from sharing letters and pictures on birthdays and holidays to being like part of the family. Sometimes they even have the birth mother, while she's pregnant, live with the adoptive family so that they can become close. We just have to work it out between the four of us. We may find the perfect family but they might not want to see us all the time. That would be hard to take. But if they are the family that we feel is best for the baby, then we'll have to sacrifice. We want some kind of contact and involvement in this child's life. We don't want it to be confusing for him. But kids can grow up with open adoption, knowing that one set of parents is raising them and they have these other parents too, who also love them. They can have the best of both worlds.

I don't exactly know what I'm going to do with the rest of my life. I have to face these drug charges and I don't know how much jail time I might get. I'm terrified about what's going to happen. I don't want to be pregnant and in jail. After this whole thing is over, I'm going to need a major change of scenery, something therapeutic. I'll either go back to school or do something productive, some kind of program. I'm still struggling between what I want to do and what other people want me to do and trying to figure out who I am. But no matter what happens, there will always be a special place for Michael inside me, always, always, always. That will never go away. I won't have children for a long time, but if I was going to have a baby, it wouldn't be with anyone else. I wouldn't be able to share with anyone else what we're sharing now with this pregnancy. When this is over, we're not saying good-bye; we're saying farewell. It's not going to be easy to go our separate ways, knowing that we deeply care for each other. We always say that we'd both be happy if we get back together someday, if that naturally evolves.

Some people see us as doing the wrong thing. We see it as allowing this child to have a life. The way we feel about each other and what we need for ourselves, it's the only way that feels natural. When I think of other young people in this same situation, I want to tell them to make sure you examine the reasons why you're in a relationship. It's one thing to be with someone because you want to be with them and another because you don't want to be alone or you want someone to love you. I don't think relationships are the only things in the world that make us happy. A lot of people forget that when you're alone, you get a chance to develop yourself. If you're pregnant and trying to decide what to do, don't let yourself be pressured by anyone. Don't move too fast; take your time and decide what is best for you. Michael and I have learned that every person in every situation has different possibilities. Don't be swayed by other people's opinions or statistics. Be true to yourself.

July 6, 1996

Court is done! I feel fortunate having been charged with only one count of delivery and sentenced to 180 hours of community service and a fine. But most importantly, we have found the perfect couple for our baby. They are from London and they have just arrived, waiting for this precious little boy to be born. It is exciting to see them, but difficult as well for this means the beginning of the end. The end of being pregnant (which I have loved so much), the end of Michael's and my relationship as lovers and constant companions, and the end of my life as I have previously known it. I seem cheerful on the outside, but when I'm alone I can hear my secret thoughts.

Michael is so excited, waiting for Joseph (that's what we've decided to name the baby) to be born. I know he loves this baby as much as I do, but I am not sure if it is as real for him as it is for me. Throughout the pregnancy we've been together, and he has given all the energy and love he has. I love him so much. I cannot believe our relationship is going to end. That in itself is more pain than anyone would want to endure. Coupled with the loss of our child, it might be more than I can take. Our families still seem to be, or are pretending to be, supportive of our choice. I wonder what they're all really thinking? Everyone is obviously bracing themselves and waiting for the pain that is inevitable.

July 26, 1996

Life has been so hectic! Joseph was born on July 11 after a long, hard labor (sixty hours), and his birth was probably easier than what has happened since then. The night before the adoption was to go into effect, Michael and I realized we needed more time to see if relinquishing Joseph was the right thing to do. Both of us were having doubts we were not vocalizing, and they were starting to come out. With this baby truly here now, we were functioning as a family, even if it was only temporary, and it dawned on us that we *could* make a life together, happily, if we really wanted to. But did we want to sacrifice a more exciting life for a family one? What about college and being young? Neither of us had been very independent yet. And what about Peter and Gilly, here all the way from England to get the child they have been waiting so long for? Not to mention Joseph himself. What was best for him? It was awful being torn in ten thousand directions at once.

Michael was ready to jump into being a parent, while I was much more hesitant, for I had been totally deliberate in my plans for this baby. I wasn't about to change my mind simply because Joseph had arrived and I loved him more than I ever thought I could love anyone. My reasons for this adoption were very real and they were still there. I had never considered keeping Joseph, ever. If we did decide to parent him, how would we do it? We

would be wonderful parents - that I never doubted. But would we be able to give Joseph everything he needed? I was scared. I did not want to become an unhappy middle-aged woman because I had had a baby too young, but as Michael said, "Joseph might delay some things a bit in our lives, but there would be other things just as wonderful to replace them." Plenty of people had children young and lead incredibly full lives. But what about being married?

Michael wanted to keep him and was totally committed to me. I still felt confused, afraid to make up my mind, fearing I would make the wrong choice and regret it for the rest of my life. I called people, wanting help, but no one could make this decision for me and I felt desperately alone.

I could not stand at this crossroads forever. I took a breath and chose. We would keep the baby!

So here we are, fifteen days after Joseph's birth. Everyone is happy, including me. I made the right choice. My only regret is that I have put everyone through so much unnecessary pain, especially Gillian and Peter. If I had only known. But that's the past. Now we have more pressing issues to think about, like our WED-DING! In one brief moment I have completely changed my destiny again, this time for the better.

March 23, 1997

This is the most peaceful and wonderful my life has ever been, although sometimes I feel a bit crazy from staying with a baby all the time. Michael has been in school at a community college and soon he starts his first quarter at the University of Washington. We are waiting to hear about family housing and financial aid. Soon, hopefully, we'll be living in the city with other young families.

I have finished my community service and, with a loan from Michael's father, I have paid my fine. I AM A FREE WOMAN! I spend my days as a full-time mom, and I am getting the hang of juggling the responsibilities of a mother and a wife. It is not always easy. Some days I am too tired to do anything except take care of Joseph, and some days even that is too much, especially when he's waking up six to eight times a night to nurse. Some days I hate Michael simply because he is a man and the baby is not as dependent on him. He is not the one getting little or no sleep. He sees other people all day long while at school and work, while I see hardly anyone. I miss people my own age. I do mourn the life of freedom that I could have had, like any other college student, but I wouldn't trade my life for anything.

Joseph is crawling, pulling himself up, talking up a storm, eating solids, and a billion other things. He is growing up so fast. Everyone is completely in love with him, and how could they not be? He is our gift from above, a blessing in disguise. This life is exactly what Michael and I needed. Everything is going in the right direction. The two of us have so many plans for ourselves and for Joseph, and slowly but surely we are putting them into action. We are more focused than we have ever been in our entire lives. Right now we are perfectly happy, building a strong foundation for the future and watching our baby grow.

The Right to Choose
Linda Wolf

Nobody *wants* to get pregnant before they're ready to, but it happens all too easily. Even though we *know* how not to, even though we may take great precautions, it still happens.

When it does, we have three choices: keep the child, give up the child, or have an abortion. All three of these require responsible thinking before we make a decision. But we should always have the right to choose.

I never imagined I would have to get an abortion, but when I got pregnant, I knew I was too young to be a mother. At the time, I didn't have enough life experience to realize what I was doing to the innocent life inside me or how it would affect me emotionally. All I knew was that I couldn't have a child right then. I believed that, because my boyfriend didn't want to get married and have a family, my only option was to have an abortion.

The first time I got pregnant, I was living in southern France with my French boyfriend. I was deeply involved in trying to make him

be 'the one,' although he was clear that he was not ready to make a commitment. We were using the rhythm method of birth control, which was not too smart. I had taken birth control pills when I first became sexually active, but they made me sick and I knew they had bad side effects. My mom told me the diaphragm was better, but I hated interrupting sex to go put it in. AIDS wasn't an issue back then, and I never had the guts to demand that guys be the responsible ones. So I got pregnant.

Because abortions were illegal then in France, we had to travel for days to cross the border into Belgium to find an abortion clinic. We found one on a side street. It was clean, the doctor was reputable, but it felt like a fast-food drive-through the way we girls were shuffled in, three at a time, hooked up without any anesthetic or painkillers, vacuumed out, and herded into a recovery room to rest before being pushed out the door.

When it was over, I remember barely being able to walk, but I was relieved not to be pregnant anymore. My womb was cramping and I was bleeding onto a pad; I felt sick and deeply, deeply sad. My boyfriend and I took the train back to Paris. I don't think we spoke during the whole ride. I'm sure he was relieved to have it over with and felt terrible for me. But I wanted to be loved, to be married, and to have a baby so badly that I soon got pregnant by him again. This time I came home to my mother in the U.S. and had the second abortion in a hospital where I was given anesthetic and a day to recuperate, as well as private care.

It was an awful time in my life. I was so lost and felt I had no one to talk to. I still hadn't come to understand why I kept getting pregnant 'accidentally.' Because I experienced what a nightmare it is to live in a country where abortions are illegal, and because I heard so many stories about what women had to do if they didn't have the money to travel out of the country as I did, I am that much more adamant today that governments, religions, institutions, and people stay out of a woman's business when it has to do with her body.

According to Barbara Walker, abortion has historically been outlawed because it was dangerous to men, not because of any worry over the fetus or mother. The early Greeks and Catholics believed that a father's semen conveyed the soul to the fetus, so if the fetus were destroyed, the father would suffer. But if the church was opposed to abortion because it killed a soul's life, it sure didn't worry about the souls of hundreds of thousands of women and men who were burned at the stake in the name of God because they were accused of being witches; often, ironically, for giving women herbs to prevent pregnancy.

Throughout history, opposition to legalizing abortion stemmed from the belief that women must be controlled by being forced to bear children. Men felt that if women were left to their own devices, they'd be having sex all the time with whomever they pleased. Not only would men not be able to control us, but they'd never know who their children were. Meanwhile, thousands of desperate pregnant women died from using coat hangers and knitting needles to do the job themselves.

In her book, *Backlash: The Undeclared War Against American Women*, Susan Faludi says that in the past decade many anti-abortion groups have organized attacks against what they call "the feminist child killers." Between 1977 and 1989, 77 family-planning clinics were torched or bombed (in at least seven instances during working hours, with employees and patients inside), 177 were targets of arson, 250 received bomb threats, 231 were invaded, and 224 vandalized. Since 1989, anti-abortion protesters have blinded, maimed, struck, choked, and murdered employees and doctors, all in the name of caring about the lives of unborn babies. The anti-abortion crusade has decreased women's future reproductive options as well by influencing politicians to cut funding for birth control research. In the 1960s, over two dozen corporations were funding birth control research on contraception; by 1990, only one remained.

We know having sex without a condom can result in an unplanned pregnancy as well as AIDS. Using condoms and spermicide will prevent pregnancy 99.9 percent of the time. Plus, it is the only method of birth control that has any ability to diminish the chances of contracting sexually transmitted diseases such as chlamydia, gonorrhea, syphilis, and others. All this information is readily available in most public middle and high schools or through family-planning centers. So why it is so many girls who know this are still getting pregnant by 'accident?' And why aren't the girls who don't know this getting the information?

While I believe it is a woman's right to choose the option of abortion - specifically in the first trimester of pregnancy- I know what an awful experience it is to endure, particularly emotionally. And while we may grow in deeply positive ways from any of our experiences, we have the power, resources and knowledge, especially in most western countries, to avoid having to make these painful choices in the first place.

For years, I felt ashamed for having abortions. After I got over that, I felt shame because I'd allowed myself to get pregnant at all. After I forgave myself, I felt ashamed that I'd been so needy for love and so lacking in self-esteem.. Ultimately I forgave myself for all of it and, recently, in a sacred healing ceremony, I buried those spirits I'd carried so long inside me under a beautiful cedar tree.

The truth I discovered is that no one can fill the gaping hole of pain I feel inside. It has to be filled by my own self love and, from that, in little ways, everyday, I'll naturally tend to choose the best for myself and ask it from others. The best we can do is try to love ourselves, be compassionate, and make the best of life, no matter what happens.

Deanna Teasley

I was just eighteen years old when I got pregnant through having unprotected sex. I was a very immature know-it-all with a chip on my shoulder, angry, insecure, and bored.

James, who was twenty-three and the first person that I ever had a real relationship with, lived across the field from me on the [Nez Perce] reservation. Everything happened very fast and I thought I could handle it. We were together for three months, engaged at six months, pregnant at eight months, and married at eleven months. I didn't know what love was as I know love now, because I had never felt it. I was going through the motions. I didn't know anything, I was just there ... in it.

For the first three months I didn't feel pregnant, until I could feel her move. I was in denial. I knew that I would never have an abortion because I would have felt guilty. We were so stupid. We thought, "Well, if we get pregnant, we get pregnant," and when we did we went, "Whoa!" When I got married, I was at the altar saying to myself, "What the fuck are you doing here?" I was this pregnant kid, getting married, and I wasn't in love.

When I was married, everything I did revolved around James's schedule and I was so totally wrapped up in his life, I didn't have my own. I didn't know how I could be without him, not because I would miss him so much but because I didn't know how to take care of myself. When I had my baby, Drea, I felt, "Wow, she's mine." I fell in love with her immediately. It was just her and me all the time, and I didn't want anyone else to watch her or hold her. I was very protective. I was home with her for fourteen months and it was great.

I was quickly becoming unhappy and I didn't know why, so I would talk myself out of it. After Drea turned a year old, I started working and meeting other people. I always knew that I wanted to travel and meet new people and see different places and this was part of what I was missing. I came home from work one day and I had this feeling in my heart that I couldn't be there anymore. I just knew. I told James I didn't love him and I didn't want to be

married anymore and live the life I was living. I wasn't growing. I was stagnant. I was living a total lie. Where we grew up, if you didn't go to school, you were supposed to get married and have kids. It wasn't James's fault; he didn't know any better either. He couldn't believe I wanted to leave. He was crying and holding Drea. I wasn't going to argue, so I left and came back a couple of days later and got my clothes.

I didn't leave because of Drea but because I was just too young and I knew I had a lot I needed to do. I didn't feel like I could take Drea with me because I didn't think that I could take care of her. I knew she was safe with James. He had a good job and our families nearby. So she stayed there. I needed to go and learn how to take care of myself and be independent, so I moved in with my girlfriend's mom. I was so used to being with James and Drea, and I was still nursing her then. I didn't sleep and I cried. I was pretty numb for a long time, though I didn't have real grief till a year later and that's when it really hit.

That was five years ago, and now I know it was the biggest mistake I ever made in my life. It's the thing that hurts me the most. I

Daughters of the Moon, Sisters of the Sun

don't like to talk about it because it brings up bad feelings and memories. I know now that I could have taken care of her. If I had the chance to do it over, I would have taken her with me. I made a lot of mistakes and I am at the point of looking back at those mistakes, feeling remorse and trying to make amends.

I haven't seen Drea in four months. It's hard to be in touch because her dad doesn't have a phone, so I call her at his work or her Aunt Sally's after school. When I lived in Seattle she was only five hours away; now that I'm in Hawaii she's half an ocean away from me. It's still great when I am with her, and I've always wanted her to be with me. Now I know I can take care of her. It will be scary but I don't have the lack of confidence that I felt five years ago. Her dad takes good care of her, but maybe now he needs to do what I did five years ago. For the most part, I think James has forgiven me. I still care for him.

As for Drea, I think she has held up pretty good. She still tells her dad that she wants him to marry me so she can be with her mom. She still doesn't understand. I don't see how I could not have hurt her. She can't tell me now, but I'm sure it will come up later. I don't for-

give myself; I just live with it. I don't think about it all the time, but I'll never not feel guilty for leaving. I think when she gets old enough and I can talk to her, I will tell her exactly what I am telling you. Maybe then, if she forgives me, I can forgive myself. I don't think I'll ever lose the guilt I feel, even when she's thirty. I will never get back the time that I am missing with her right now.

I felt then that I knew so much and was going to conquer the world. I look back on myself now and I think, "You were so stupid and so young. You knew nothing." There I was, trying to play like I knew what I was actually doing. Kids think they know everything, but they don't. I was a kid having a kid. When I was playing around with sex at eighteen, I wasn't even enjoying it. I didn't have an orgasm till I was twenty-three. I was wondering what all the hype was about. I remember thinking, "What's the big deal? This isn't that great." I think the only reason I enjoy sex now is that I know how to please myself first. I know what I need and I can show my partner what to do.

Even now I am young, but wiser than I was then. I know that I would love to have another baby, but I know that now is not the time because there are things I have to do before I have another child. I don't want to look back and say, "I wish I would have done this or that." Not that a child isn't a blessing, but it takes money to take care of them and give them a good home.

I do everything I can not to get pregnant; I use condoms and I have an IUD. I want more children and I want to get married. I never thought I'd say that, but I definitely see it in my future after I get my first degree from college. A couple of years ago I thought I was pregnant and went into an abortion clinic. I remember the doctor telling me what the procedure was and I thought, "I can't do this." Luckily for me I wasn't pregnant. I don't think there is anything wrong with abortion, but for me, I'd feel so guilty because I know that nine months later comes this beautiful baby.

I would advise other young women to do everything they can not to get pregnant. Wait until you are ready emotionally and physically. If you are pregnant and feel trapped and don't have an income, move back in with your parents or go on welfare or take a technical course. Take anything. It would be hard, but you have to do what you have to do to survive. If you have a baby, it will be that much more to push you. Today I would tell a girl to take her child with her. It may take some learning and take some time, but you can do it on your own. I would tell her, "Never leave your child, take your child."

I want Drea to know that I did all that I could do at the time. I want her to be happy and follow her heart, do what's right for her and not let anyone tell her differently. I can't imagine loving anyone as much as I do her. She'll be my baby till I die. She'll be 100 and I'll be 118 and she'll still be my baby. She's the best thing I've ever done or created. She's pretty amazing.

Kids Having Kids

Wind Hughes

It was New Year's Eve, December 31, 1969. I was married and in labor, about to give birth to my first child, Kimberly.

I was fifteen years old and beside myself with the joy and wonder of giving birth and becoming a parent. People often stared or gasped when they heard my age. You should have seen the nurses at the hospital calling each other into the room to see the "young mom." Actually, they were rather rude. There's a social stigma to being a teen parent, a shaming.

Parenting came naturally and easily to me. I loved being a mom, nursing, changing diapers, going for walks with Kimberly in her stroller, holding her in my arms and marveling at this tiny being. She was a joy in my life, my buddy, and we went everywhere together. I called her Little Biddle or Kimberly Bimberly Bop.

I was a very happy and strong person. My mother had always told me that I could do anything I set my mind to; it's a good thing I believed her because hard times were coming. When Kimberly was about one and a half, I became a statistic: a divorced teen mom on welfare. One half of all teen mothers in the United States are on welfare within the first year of giving birth; 75 percent within five years. In 1992, the U.S. government reported that close to half of all single women on welfare were teen mothers, and every year the numbers rise.

I knew this wouldn't work for me as a lifestyle, so at seventeen I completed my General Education Diploma and entered college. I never could have imagined, nor would I have believed anyone who tried to warn me, of the long-term consequences of teen parenting. As difficult as things were, I was happy, enjoyed my independence, and was proud of being in college.

Kimberly's dad left the country and didn't help financially. (According to the Casy Foundation, only 40 percent of families headed by teen moms get financial help from the father.) I was broke and I made some desperate choices in the name of survival, in the name of food. You do things you'd never imagine when you need to feed your child.

Those days, in New York City, you were not allowed to attend college while on welfare, so I was told I had to drop out of school and report to the employment office and look for work. It was about then that I began to feel I was living my life with my hands tied behind my back. I couldn't afford childcare, I was too young to make enough money in any job to properly support the two us, and I didn't want to stay on welfare all of my life. I was told I could stay on welfare until my children were grown, but I couldn't stay in school. Go figure. I often felt that the system was working against me, not for me.

I refused to drop out of school, but I did report to the employment office and prayed that they would never find me a job. Then one day an angel, disguised as a feminist social worker, took a liking to me and arranged for my file to be, let's say, cleared, so I was able to stay in college and to continue my education. I was given a chance. The ties on my hands were loosened just enough to enable me to eventually leave the life of welfare behind.

I'll never forget the day my daughter and I left Brooklyn on our way to our new life in California. As I watched the tenement I lived in fade, I felt a pang of sadness - survivor's guilt - for all of the other single moms I was leaving behind to their own destiny. How many of them would never find an angel and would remain on welfare? It's a hopeless way of living. I still cringe inside when I hear someone make the statement that a woman is having more kids so she can get more welfare. Hellllloooo?!

Many teen parents feel the social stigma: "She must have been a bad girl since she obviously was having sex so young!" They internalize this sense of shame and it grows even

larger as poverty takes hold. You hear many messages about how your life is ruined, you'll never finish school, you'll probably be poor most of your life - and statistically, it's probable. I have worked with enough teen parents to know that in many ways my case is unusual. Remember, I had an angel, relentless motivation, a very mellow child, a love of parenting, and deep spiritual beliefs that gave my life meaning. Not every young parent fares so well.

I remarried, continued college, and at twenty-one had my second child, a son, Justin. He was always pointing to everything, wanting to know what it was, saying, "Dis, dis?" So we called him Baba Dis. I was in heaven, living in the mountains, happy, loving being a mom, being married, being stable, having enough food.

I was twenty-seven when the strain of early parenting began to show up in my life. It was all catching up with me. I began to feel unsettled in my marriage and can see now that I hadn't had enough time alone for my own self-development. I got divorced while I was still in graduate school.

The years of financial stress began again.

Since I had been the one in our relationship who stayed home with the kids most of the time, I had slowed down my academic advancement and the building of a viable income of my own. It took me a long time to get through college and graduate school: eleven years. Many things seemed so much harder for me than for women who had not had kids so young.

The hardest part for me was not the parenting but the financial stress that came with it. Statistics from the Guttmacher Institute show that teenage mothers are more at risk of economic disadvantage *throughout their lives* than those who delay childbearing until their twenties. I still see that impact in my life today. When you are a teen parent, you need a lot of energy to get through the long haul. It's a catch-22; you have to develop and educate yourself so that you can take care of a family while the family is already there. Everything has to be done at once - NOW! This is why so many teen parents, especially single teen parents, don't get through high school, college, or vocational training. It's too much to take on *at once.*

The Guttmacher Institute also says that three out of every four teenagers who have a baby did not plan the birth, and one in three teen parents have another baby within two years. It's important to be the creator of your own destiny, not a victim of circumstance. I was so young when I became sexually active, and I didn't have a clue what I was doing. I enjoyed the closeness and intimacy and that's what I think I most wanted at that age. My pregnancy wasn't planned, but we weren't using birth control either. We had a fantasy about life together and if we got pregnant ... then we would have this beautiful child. Well, we had the beautiful child, but the fantasy did not unfold as imagined.

I believe many young women are looking for intimacy, connection and closeness in a society where many of us feel alienated from each other. The divorce rate is high and the extended family and our sense of community are disintegrating. The value of intimate relationships has been replaced with the desire for financial wealth and the drive to consume. It seems that for many young people, sex is becoming a way to meet the need for intimacy and for love.

Also, girls are victimized by a culture

that sexualizes them and then condemns them for being sexual, a culture where a large measure of a girl's self-worth is determined by her appearance. Movies and music videos are full of sexualized, very young girls. Our culture encourages young women to be sexual, to be like what they see in the media, but gives them little information on sexuality - budget cuts to women's health-care and prevention programs are decreasing the availability of affordable health care, birth control, and information on sex.

What a mixed message we are giving young women: feel good about yourself, but only if you have the right kind of body. Be sexual, but we'll reduce the availability of information you need to avoid pregnancy. If you do get pregnant, don't have an abortion. But if you have the child and decide to keep it, you won't be eligible for welfare unless you remain dependent upon your parents or an institution. Damned if you do and damned if you don't.

If you already are a young mother, don't let go of your dreams and goals no matter how difficult the situation may seem. I have found that there is always a way to create what we need. It may not be apparent *how* at the moment, and it may not happen in the time frame that we'd like, but a solution is out there. Be creative and believe in yourself.

My children have been my biggest teachers in all ways, especially teaching me love and selflessness. I would never trade my life with them for anything. Being so close in age to my kids has always felt like a gift. I was young enough to enjoy them, play with them, hang out with them. In some ways we grew up together. One of our favorite family activities has been going to concerts - we actually listen to the same music.

It's strange when people who meet me now are surprised to hear I have children. They are living on their own and are not around a lot, but they have been so much a part of my life. As with everything in life, things change, even parenting. Raising children takes only a short period of our lives. It goes quickly. Very quickly. So here I am with adult kids who are my best friends, and I have many years ahead of me, still young enough to enjoy them and my future. Looking back, it was a struggle, a hard struggle. Here and now, what a blessing!

Kimberly Hoffman

My mother, Wind, gave birth to me when she was fifteen years old. I am twenty-seven now and we are still very close.

I have memories of going everywhere with my mom when I was little, even to college, and I have such good impressions and feelings from those memories. My mom always wore a cape and I remember I would huddle under it all of the time, like a mother duck and her baby duckling. I felt very safe.

I never felt a lack of having a father

because my stepdad was my father since I was four. But I did feel a sense of abandonment by my biological father. As a child, I couldn't understand how he could not want to love me or be with me after my parents got divorced. He didn't spend much time with me and then he left the country. I've only seen him two or three times since I was three, and when I did it was uncomfortable. I have a closer relationship with my grandparents (his parents) since they have always stayed in contact with me.

As I got older, I couldn't understand how he could not want to be in my life. I wasn't looking for him to create a family because I already had a family, but I was beginning to take his absence personally. I remember wondering what I did to him: "Was I so horrible that he didn't even want to talk to me?" My mom helped me with those feelings because I was really angry about it. She had me sit down and write him a letter explaining how I felt, and I felt better after I sent it. He never responded to it. The one time I spoke to him after the letter, I didn't care anymore. I think those feelings had a lot to do with some of my struggles as a teenager.

When I look back on my life now, one of the things I am most grateful for is that I never felt a lack of love from my mother. She was always there for me and I always knew where I belonged. I had a strong mother and we had a strong bond.

When I was little, I didn't have a clue my mom was so young. I began to realize it when I was older and friends would see her and ask, "How old is your mother? She looks so young." I was always proud of that. She was so young and beautiful and she was my mom. I remember loving to tell people how young she was because I thought it was cool; not that I wanted to have kids that young, but more because she was such a great mom and we were so close. I still think it's cool.

I don't think having children so young would be the best choice for most people, and life was probably harder because she made that choice. I've thought that she could have had an abortion and I'm glad she had me instead. I respect that choice, but only because she handled it properly. Lots of young people have kids and I don't think they handle it well. She still carried on her life. She went to school, educated herself, and did the best she could. She could have had me and abandoned

me and done drugs. I could have grown up more of a hippie kid than I did. With all that happened, I feel I've grown up well and I thank God she didn't make a different choice. If I had been pregnant at fifteen, I probably would have had an abortion. There's no way I was mature enough at fifteen, and I'm probably still not at my age.

Both of my parents were of the sixties culture and I think when I was young I was resentful that I didn't have more fundamental parents. In grade school I was more of a hippie kid. When I was in sixth grade, all the other girls wore make-up and dressed really pretty. They were more 'girls.' Their mothers were into more traditional feminine roles and my mom wasn't. So at times I felt out of place.

As I got older, my mom and I would do lots of things together and sometimes I would hang out at home with her and her friends, which I think, in part, is why I matured so quickly. I think that's when our closeness in age caused some problems. When it came time for boundaries, we had more difficulty. I couldn't understand why I couldn't do the things I wanted to, since I felt older than I was, and I couldn't understand some of the restrictions. We did everything together, we hung out and went to concerts together, so when I wanted to do these things on my own, it would be hard when she'd be in the mom role and say no.

When you are a kid, everything is so important to you. I wanted to stay out till 1 a.m. I wondered how come I could go to concerts with her and stay out late, but I couldn't do it with my friends? I didn't understand that I was fifteen. I was trying to grow up so quickly. Maybe that's because she was so young and it was a youthful household. I have always respected her as my mother. I never felt like,

"Oh this is my sister." She was definitely always my mom.

I hated my high school years. We lived in Carmel Valley, California, and we were poor and I was surrounded by people who were so rich. They could have things and do things I couldn't. I didn't have a big beautiful house. We had a cool house, but I didn't have what other people had. For a while I was sharing a room with my brother and he was very difficult. I wanted to be a teenager, and here was this kid with me. I didn't have enough privacy. That was a consequence of living with a single parent. We were so broke. I could have lived with dad and had more of a material life, but I chose not to. When I was fourteen and fifteen years old, it was a hard time for us. I hated it. The economics really impacted me.

I hope that I don't have to raise my kids alone. I realize that sometimes there's no other choice. I guess I feel that mom had a choice and maybe she gave up on her marriage to my stepdad too easily and it could have been different. We could have all gone to counseling. Maybe not. I don't know. It's confusing. I do resent some of the choices she made. I wish the family could have stayed together. I can be angry about it, but in some ways I understand.

It's an illusion to think that if you hide things from your kids, then they won't do what you do. But I do think you need to be careful of how much you share with them. I don't want my kids to feel like they can't talk to me about things or know what I did in my life. I definitely want open channels of communication. Yet I don't want them to feel like it's okay to party like I partied. It wasted a lot of my time. When I was partying, I was so adamant that I didn't want to be in school or do sports or other things that were good for me. But now, looking back, I feel like I made a big error because I have had to live with the consequences.

I am thankful, as a whole, that I was raised the way I was, because we have done things and shared experiences together that most people don't get to do with their parents, and it has created a bond and a friendship between my mother and me that I don't think we would have had otherwise. I value that very much and if I have children, I would like to raise them that way also.

I think it's important to talk with your

kids as much as you can. I told my mom almost everything and she didn't judge me, so I always knew that there was someone there for me, even when I didn't think I wanted her to be. I look back and even with all the things I complain about and the times that were hard, she never stopped working and educating herself. I respect her for that because I don't think I could have done it at that age. As a kid, I didn't realize that. I don't know how she went to school and did it all. I find it difficult *now* in my life. She worked hard to keep the balance of work and time with us. Even though some of the decisions she made I don't think were the right ones, it doesn't matter because I love her and we are so close. I know my mother is the strongest person I've ever met.

I think young people need to be kids and experience what young people experience. But sex is not worth the risk. Use contraception or wait! I've never gotten pregnant and I'm thankful not to have had to make that choice. It's funny, but if I had to tell teen parents what to do, I'd probably tell them to do what my mother did with me. She always loved me and cared and made sure that I knew she was there for me. It's confusing because there are things I think could have been different, but at the same time she obviously gave me the tools, the strength, and the knowledge to help me make my life as successful as it is now.

FOUR

FINDING OUR POWER

Jessi Old Coyote

The most important thing to me is my family. My parents, Steve and Rita, my sisters, Janaka and Alyssum, my brother, James, and his son, Bearon.

Me and my mom, we pretty much run our whole house. My mom is the one who takes care of the kids. She's the one who deals with all the hardships and stands by her man's side. My dad is expected to make the money. Whenever he can't get us money, he is really down on himself and feels stressed and struggles even more than my mom does. I don't know who's stronger in the Native American culture because the self-esteem of the majori-ty of our people on both sides, male or female, is really low. You either have people whose self-esteem is really low and who are struggling every day of their life just to try and stand up, or people whose self-esteem is really high and they know they can do it and they go out and do it. But I've never seen a rich Native American.

What I want for my life is a good job, a big house, a nice car, and I want to go to school. I know I'm gonna have to fight pretty much my whole life to get close to where I want to be because of who I am, because of where I live, and because I'm a minority. But when I succeed, I'll use my life to show others that they can do it too.

A lot of people in my community don't believe it's possible to get out of their situation. I was talking to a guy last night who thought everything was impossible. I sat for three hours out in front of my house in his car, telling him that it's not impossible. I told him over and over in different words that he can't give up. In life you have to be strong in who you are. All his life goals are based on showing the majority that he is bigger than them, that he's more powerful, and that he would die proving it. I told him that it just shows he's weak and that they can get him. I felt like my mom and dad saying that to him, because I said the exact same things that they said to me when I was feeling like him, and he was saying the exact same things that I used to say to them. But I know how he feels. It's just because, ever since you're born, white people have always fucked with you. They're always on top. Like the Tribal Center - it's white run. The director is a white man. And the bingo hall and the casino; it's all white run. That's why we don't ever go there. Just knowing the history of things white people did to my people in the past, like cutting babies' heads off and stuff like that, pisses me off, but I have to understand it's the past and I can't dwell on it.

Yet every single day I walk down the street, I'm looked at. If I go into a store, I'm followed. If me and my friend Nikki go into a store, they will follow me, not her, because she looks white. I used to try to fight it off, to get them back. But I let that go a long time ago. The only way I learned to deal with it was to understand where they were coming from and why they treated me that way. They're ignorant. I know what I want in my life and I'm not going to let nobody stop me. I want to help my people, the Native American people. I have to keep strong inside to get through it or else I'll get nowhere. I think the only way we can heal things is when we acknowledge what happened.

I identify with being Native American mostly, although ever since I was in the Girls Focus Group and listened to all the other girls' stories, I've started thinking about the fact that we're all alike. We women are just now trying to get a voice in our own community. It's a struggle. It's like the same old roles where the man is the man and the woman is the woman. For example in the Native American church, women have to wear skirts and have their hair fixed, but the men can go in their dirty old jeans and an old shirt. In my family right now, we're noticing all this and we're standing up to it. And we're letting them know that they can't push us around with their egos anymore. If we have to wear skirts to church and do this and that, then they have to wear their ribbon shirts and their nice pants.

It wasn't always this way. When you look back into the history of our people, it's the women who were the medicine people. It was a woman who brought the peace pipe, it was the woman who was usually the priest, and it was a woman who found peyote and brought it to our people. It's like we are looking back on our history and learning things and trying to figure out where it changed – where and when did the man feel like he has to put his ego on us? At first nobody wanted to mention these things, but we're talking about it all now.

And another thing that we don't like is that in our meetings and in our ceremonies, the men say that we can't be there when we're on our periods. We can't have our periods and be in a sweat, or they make these rules like whenever you have your period, you can't hold an eagle feather, or whenever you have your period, you can't do this and you can't do that.

That's one of the reasons I don't participate in the Native American church anymore. I told them it's because they're all a bunch of hypocrites. I told them, "You sit in there and talk about how pure you are and how spiritual you are, and when you're done you go out and smoke some weed - you guys look like a bunch of hypocrites." I talked to them about all the rules women are made to follow that the men don't have to and asked them how come a woman has to have so many restrictions on her? A guy can go drunk to church and they let him participate. It just pissed me off. It's like the male ego came in and took over and ever since we started looking back, it's gotten all jumbled up. Now everybody is questioning what is real and what isn't, what we can believe and what we can't, what they should be praying for, who they should be praying to, and who they should be praying with? I told my uncle that when the day comes that all this has straightened out, I'll come back.

I also know now that women experience the same kind of violence in the Native American culture as anywhere. But here, the women are tough, too; they'll fight back. They don't just let themselves get beat up. They get beat up one day, but the next they might come in and kick the guy's ass in his sleep. It's just like on every other reservation; you'll see the same old thing going on and on: the mom and dad beating each other up and the kids pretty much living on their own. A lot of the men who do this are always drunk, they are always down at the bars. Every now and then I'll go down to the bars and if I see people that I recognize or that I know, I'll say, "What are you doing here? Why don't you go home and feed your kids? Go do something." They just laugh and say, "Oh Jessi," and give me some excuse. I say, "No, I'm serious, I'm not joking around." Most of the time they don't remember it. They just go back into the bar.

When I see kids' parents down at the bar, I'll go to the house to make sure the kids are okay, or I'll call them and make sure they have food, make sure they're not hungry. If I see them down at the store, I'll buy them some candy or whatever makes them happy. On my reservation, all the kids call me Big Sister. Sometimes they'll stop by to see me - that makes me happy. I want them all to know that they have somebody that will listen to them, somebody that will be there for them. I get involved because I choose to get involved, because I see them as my family. A lot of other people won't look, they'll just go home. But not me. I'll jump right in there, even if I get hit - I'll jump right in there and take that kid out of the problem. I'll do whatever I can to save that kid from getting hit again. I'll bring kids home sometimes. I'll say, "Mom, we got a new kid." They stay for a couple of days until they want to go back home.

I'm not angry with my people; I'm sad for them. I wish I could take each one of them and shake all their anger and hatred out of them, because that's what brings them down. But I can't. I know I can't change it all in my lifetime and I know that my sisters can't change it all in their lifetimes. There's so many of us and so many things that have happened. It's not like you can get us together all at once and teach us all at the same time. We have to change things a little bit at a time every single day. We have to teach little by little by little by little, because we have all these people who are so angry. They let that anger hold them back and use that anger as an excuse or reason to be fucked up, and it gets them stuck and they can't move on and they keep going around in a circle. I used to be stuck in that circle. I used to just hate people so much. I had so much anger built up inside me and my parents had to keep talking to me and keep telling me the same thing over and over and over again until I saw, until I understood, that I can't let that anger bring me down.

A lot of people look up to me and ask me how I stay so strong. I come from a family of strong people. My mom, my dad - everybody looks up to them. They're representatives in our community. Just listening to them and doing what they taught me has made me pretty much a representative, too. When I was little, I remember my grandpa and my uncles and my grandma and my aunties always telling me that they could see I had a voice, that I'd be one to help change the cycle, change all this bullshit. And they told me that if I would just sit and listen to myself and connect with myself and my culture, my religion, I was going to see it all and be able to talk and teach people. Every day I would look for that to happen and I would wonder where it is. Just recently it has started to come to me.

I think you have to have patience and understanding for everybody. I think when we experience prejudice, we have to stop and think about where it's coming from, why people do it, and just move on. We have to understand it. You have to understand who taught them to be prejudiced, where they learned it from. I remember this TV show I saw where this woman had her little baby dressed up in a Ku Klux Klan suit. Just a brand new baby. That baby is going to grow up being KKK and that's all he'll ever know, and you have to remember that it came from his parents, not from him. We're all human. Every single human has a story that he or she has lived, and in order to get past it all, you have to understand, you have to know his story. That's the only way I see that we can get by and keep going.

Jessi Old Coyote talks with Wilma Mankiller

Wilma Mankiller was the first woman to serve as principal chief of the Cherokee Nation of Oklahoma. In 1970, she participated in the Alcatraz Island occupation. She is the author of the best-selling book Mankiller: A Chief and Her People.

Jessi: Who are your women role models and what did they teach you?

Wilma: There were a number of them, both Native and non-Native. My aunt was what we called an 'Indian Doctor.' Other tribes call them 'medicine people.' She doctored people and she had special dreams. I was fascinated by her. She had an influence on me at an early age.

There was a Klamath woman named Justine who had a tremendous impact on me. Other people saw Justine as an alcoholic but, God, I liked her. I didn't have much confidence then. I was living in a housing project and kind of like a street kid. Justine saw potential in me and always talked to me like I had important things to say. I felt really important because she trusted me to babysit for her children. She took me under her wing, and when I was a young adult volunteering for the Indian center and still with little confidence, she talked me into going to college. Nobody in my family or my community went to college.

In the white world there's an artist named Georgia O'Keefe. I really liked her because I didn't know many women in my world that did anything they darn well pleased, and this woman did. She lived where she wanted to, painted what she wanted to paint, said what she wanted to say, and I didn't know women like that.

Jessi: What is the legacy you think you'll leave the world?

Wilma: That there are female ways of leading and just because I was soft-spoken, that doesn't mean I couldn't get things done. Sometimes people think that leaders have to be loud or bang on tables to exercise power. But I had real power and I used that real power to build clinics and Head Start centers [for early childhood education], to do a lot of things I wanted.

At first it was tempting to adopt a more male form of leadership because people understood that. I was head of a police force and talked to the U.S. Congress and I once had a staff of 1,400 people. I had this idea that you could be the boss and do things differently. I think that it was hard at first because they wouldn't take me seriously when I would tell them to do something because I said it in a soft-spoken way. Then they were totally shocked when I would carry out what I said I would do. They were used to someone coming in and saying, "I'm the boss. Here are the directives and you follow them." For a lot of women leaders, it's easier to just become like men.

I hope I did that most of the time with a good mind and a positive attitude. I still live in the same rural poor community, and I could be overwhelmed by the number of problems here and be depressed if I focused on them. What I do instead is focus on the positive, on what is good about our people. When I start to be dragged down, I continue to focus on the positive. Other people will probably remember me for development and building programs, because that's my skill.

Someone once called me the ultimate cheerleader and I am because I believe that if we do things together, there's hope. My favorite thing to do now is to talk to young women about leadership. Goodness, if I could do it, anyone can. I took a long time to go from a girl in a housing project with no confidence to someone who, many years later, was able to step up and say, "I can lead and I want you all to vote for me."

Jessi: As a woman, how do you feel about yourself?

Wilma: I am really happy to be a woman. Women like myself who choose to live our lives differently from other women, we pay for that in many ways because we are not following the stereotype of what society expects a woman to be. We don't dress or look like other women, we don't think like other women, we don't walk like other women, and we refuse to live like many other women. We're not going to let society define what women can and cannot do. And for that we pay, sometimes by not being able to spend as much time with our families or not having deep personal relationships with men. It's a very different life. I couldn't have lived another life. This is who I am. It certainly has been difficult at times to make the choices that I did, but I am really glad that I did. I have no regrets. I truly, strongly believe, like the old Cherokees believe, that there should be balance in our communities. We should hear the women's voices and we should hear the men's voices. Men and women both have things they can contribute to leadership. Things are horribly out of balance. As a woman, I feel like I have done what I can to get the message out that we need more women in leadership.

Linda: What were women's roles in the past and how did they change with the coming of

European culture?

Wilma: In our tribe, balance was critical. We believed that the entire world existed in a precarious balance and that wrong or incorrect actions caused the world to tumble out of balance. One of the ways that things were balanced was that women and men both held power in the daily social and economic life of the tribe. Women played a prominent role. There was a women's council and they were consulted in matters of importance to the tribe. When men and women married, the man went to the woman's place. If something happened to the relationship, the woman kept the property, which was very different than what was going on in the surrounding European communities where not only did men control all the property, but women were seen as property. Over time, women assumed a more secondary role because of sexism. About the time I was running for office in 1983, our own people were saying, "We can't have a woman in office. We'll be the laughingstock of all the tribes." They forgot their own history.

Linda: I've heard you refer to ceremonial grounds. What are they?

Wilma: To me it's a sacred ground. A place where we go for different ceremonies. When you walk into that, it's like stepping into tribal tradition and forward into the future at the same time. It's an incredible feeling to hear songs that have been sung since the beginning of time and to be able to participate in a dance that women ancestors forever have been involved in. It's what helped me keep my feet on the ground. I could go from meeting one of the presidents and then go home and shed all that and put on my shells and head for the ceremonial ground and be with the women. I like the sense of solidarity by dancing with the women.

Wind: Given your background and your mom being Irish, how do you feel about the white community taking on many of your traditions?

Wilma: I think there has been too much exploitation of tribal ceremonies. You wouldn't believe how much gibberish is out there by people who claim to be medicine people. They take pieces and put it together in an odd way and publish the most ridiculous writings. It's really exploitative and shocking. It's very important now for Native people ourselves to revitalize our traditions and reclaim them. We need to go through that process before we can even talk about talking and sharing that with anyone else. There may be a time in the future when the elders gather and say to do this, but this is not the time.

Native American spirituality is not about a particular ceremony or language; it's more about how one lives one's life. Old Cherokee thought says everything has to be in balance and so it has to be in your life. You can't take one part out, one ceremony. It has to be a complete immersion. In order to do that, you almost have to suspend everything you know and start over.

Jessi: We are involved in the Native American church. Some white people will come and sit through a meeting all night, and then the next day they try to portray themselves as a Native American. My mom says these people come in and do our ceremony and it is something they do. But our ceremonies are who we *are.*

Wilma: That's an excellent way of putting it. I may quote you. How do you keep yourself positive?

Jessi: My whole life, my mom and dad have told me to be strong in who I am and to love myself. I know a lot of people who can't say they love themselves. One day I got really down on my people. Everything was overwhelming, like seeing my people drunk in the bars. I wrote my parents a letter and said I didn't want to be who I was anymore. I hated them for having me in this world. Then my mom and I had a talk and she said, "There are a lot of Native Americans out there who do love themselves, so think about those people. The people in the bars, try to help them. Believe in yourself. Believe in who you are."

Janet McCloud

*J*anet has been an activist and organizer for Native American struggles since the early 1950s and is a well-loved and highly respected elder. She was born into the Tulalip Indian tribe in 1934. She is the co-founder of the Survival of the American Indian Association and the Northwest Indian Women's Circle, and co-organizer of the Indigenous Women's Network. Janet now lives in Yelm, Washington, where she co-founded the North American Indian Lodge and the Sapa Dawn Center.

Daughters of the Moon, Sisters of the Sun

When I was younger, I didn't identify with white or black feminists because they had different issues from Native women. There was a United Nations conference on women in the media, bringing together women from all over the world. They didn't have any Native American indigenous women from North America, so they invited me. I went all prepared to talk about the oppression of Native women. There were women from Egypt, Africa, and other third world countries, and they began to relate their struggles with things I hadn't heard of before, like clitorectomies on young girls and widowed women being thrown on the cremation fire and burned with their dead husbands. I thought, "Goodness sakes, we don't have anything like that. Our struggle is actually with the white paternalistic bureaucracy." When I listened to the struggles of these women around the world, I began to see that we weren't the only women who were oppressed in the world and that we needed to find a way to come together and overcome the things that divide us, whether it's miles, religion, politics, or history.

In the late sixties and seventies, some of the major issues for Native American women were sterilization, poverty, sexism, and discrimination. The United States government sterilized roughly 40 percent of all childbearing Indian women at that time, as well as Indian women in Central and South America. It was genocide. I was involved with the Citizens Advocate, a watchdog organization in Washington, D.C., that was documenting what was happening with Native peoples. They did a project on hunger in the U.S. and discovered that of the eight major geographical hunger areas, five of them were Indian reservations. So our people were amongst the poorest, and Indian women were at the bottom of the poverty chain.

We struggled with sexism, not only from the white bureaucracy, white police, and social service workers, but also by Indian men. A lot of women were abandoned by the fathers of their children. At that time the women weren't going to college, so we had to work hard on empowerment and self-development. Now women have become very visible and leaders as well. There have been a lot of changes. I attribute the changes to the grassroots organizing that we did. Other women and I traveled all over this country, talking to and organizing women. We tried to get rid of the squaw stereotype. There's still a lot of need to work with women, but now it's not as critical.

Traditionally, our society was a feminist society because the Earth was the mother, feminine; the moon was the grandmother, feminine; and the men knew that women were the creators of life. They knew they came from a woman. Women were leaders at that time and your qualifications were that you were a human being. There was a lot more respect for women than there ever was in white society, where women were owned by their men. When the missionaries came from Europe, they would not meet in council if there were women present.

Everyone is a part of nature. We are all the children of the same mother Earth and the grandmother moon and sun. We are all living under those laws and we have to find out about those living, sacred laws. Our philosophy of life is universal. It's not rigid. As Chief Seattle said, "It's not written with the iron finger of an angry God upon tablets of stone." Ours was never that way. Ours was a free, fluid kind of spirituality where each person was responsible for their own spiritual well-being. I see all the Earth changes that are happening in the world: we, the planet, are in the process of the purification now.

I am a grandma mentor and I teach that life is a gift and that it can be beautiful or ugly depending on what you make it. You have to understand that you are free to make that decision. If you think things are not right, then you have to work to change them. You have to take your little piece of the world that needs to be worked on and do the best that you can, whatever it is. I always teach that if you change yourself and become the kind of person that you think everybody else should be, then you have changed half the world. You have to start small, at the beginning, and that's yourself. Bring out the beauty and see that that beauty is in yourself.

Tasha Flournoy

I don't see myself as black or African American. I see myself as a human being. I've always loved people, especially people who were different than me. I've always felt like I fit in, but not in the world that society has created. The only time I haven't is when other people bring it up or look at me like I'm different.

I grew up not knowing much about racism. My mother never talked to me about prejudice or told me about things such as slavery and hate crimes. It wasn't necessary; she taught me to see people for who they are and to judge them by their personality and their behavior.

I grew up in an upper-middle-class neighborhood in California with my mother, my stepfather, who was white, and my brother by their marriage. I never lived with my real father, and my mother doesn't talk about him much. They were never married. He was one of the only black men my mother was ever with. I don't think she deliberately set out to be with racially mixed men, but this was a part of her philosophy of diversity. Some African American men in her life let her down, just like my real dad let me down. I've been let down and abandoned by a lot of men in my life.

My stepfather abused me both physically and emotionally. At first he was nice, loving, and warm, but he changed overnight. Sometimes he'd be so harsh I'd get sick to my stomach. He was paranoid about my mother, always telling me that she was cheating on him. I was afraid of his temper. He would just

snap. I used to hide in my closet and write poetry to get away from him and to deal with my own feelings of anger. I remember crouching over my brother to protect him when he would hit on us.

One night I remember him screaming at my six-year-old brother about all the bills and all the problems he had with my mother, and I didn't think my brother needed to hear those things. So I went up to him and told him to stop, but he came swinging at me so I grabbed my brother and ran to the phone. I called 911 and told them my stepfather's going to hit me. When the police came I remember standing outside on the driveway and falling down on my knees. I couldn't stop crying and shaking and saying, "I can't take this anymore." We left that night.

They got divorced after that and we moved to an apartment, but things kept going downhill from there. My mother lost job after job and was divorced twice before I was thirteen, but she has always been a fighter. She taught me that there was a spiritual way to get through the hard things. It was she who taught me how to meditate and to use creative visualization and to think positively. I learned

Daughters of the Moon, Sisters of the Sun

to follow what my intuition tells me. It's different from instinctual because I'm not in a struggle or conflict with this feeling. It's a part of me that I have faith in, like my mother's strength. Sometimes now I wake up in the middle of the night and feel my mother's presence next to me. She's one of the most important people in my life. She's been my best friend and confidant all these years. All my life she has told me that I'm beautiful and special. Her words have gotten me through a lot.

My grandmother is part Native American. When she was younger, she had long, straight, black hair and could go out in the rain and not worry about it 'kinking up.' Yet we were like most black families where 'good' hair meant assimilation. It had gotten to a point where it was looked down upon to even appear in public with naturally kinky, coarse, black hair such as mine and my mother's. It was thought that if you wore short or thick naturals, you'd look like a man. Our hair is nothing like my grandmother's. We have to go through agonizing pain, burning and scabbing our scalps, to achieve the beauty of straight hair through pressing, perming, hot combing, or relaxing it. Until now I haven't thought much about this

because it was worth the pain and struggle as long as one achieved the success of 'goodness.' It's such a metaphor for the plight of black people in this country. Both black *and* white society reinforces this stereotype by objectifying black hair, and then families like mine internalize it. This idealized white form of 'black beauty,' which has been established over time, is a mask transforming the real beauty that is my crown, a beauty that it has taken me over a decade to realize.

I don't trust men very much. My father, who it's likely I'll never see again, has a lot to do with that. I can't relate to older men. I don't know what to say to them. Some of this uncomfortableness is also due to the two molestations by older boys I experienced as a child. Over the past year and a half I've done a lot of healing through my relationship with my boyfriend, Anthony. He's helped me open up a lot more to trust men again. When I first met him, he told me he babysat these two little girls and had a very special relationship with them. I was shocked. I'd never met any guy who babysat girls or who cared about children. I'd never met any male who liked children or had a special relationship with

them, who didn't hurt them. After asking him a lot of questions, I asked him point-blank if he had ever touched them or felt like touching them. He was really shocked. He told me that he'd never, ever thought of them that way.

I love being in a loving relationship that happens to be interracial. It's something special and magical. Sometimes we get dirty looks or comments from people on the street; some people yell slurs out of their cars at us. Even at school, at 'liberal' Sarah Lawrence College, we've experienced prejudice. At first a lot of the African American females looked at me like, "What is she doing with him?" Some people would say, "Why don't you stay with your own race?" Some wonder why I don't go to an all-black college, too. What they and the outside world have to say is of no importance to me.

Whenever I see interracial couples, I love them so much because I know these people are making an effort to be together. I know they must really love each other because they have to tolerate the intolerance in this world. If there were more biracial children, there would be more love in the world. If we all intermarried, there wouldn't be a reason for racism. You couldn't discriminate against anybody because they'd be just like you. That's what we need to learn anyway. People are really just us in another form. If we love them, we love ourselves.

I love myself but it's hard for me to say that. It sounds like I'm putting myself in the spotlight and I don't like to do that. But I like myself. I'm a good person. I know who I am and where I want to go. I listen to my heart and my intuition and take a lot of time to think about my decisions. I'm always asking questions, always wondering about other places, other worlds. I constantly, more like incessantly, talk and crave verbal stimulation from many people.

I love being a woman. I am a sensual being who has learned to look in the mirror and feel my legs, my face, my breasts, and say "I love you." Our problem as women is that we aren't allowed to have our sexuality out there. We can do it if we're selling something like in an ad, but if I wanted to dress sexy, I'd get gawked at or called a slut. I have to watch everything I do or say or it can be misconstrued. It's almost like I have to search out my environment before I choose which mask to put on. Like chameleons, women must adapt to their surroundings, but now I realize that my surrounding is the body I inhabit. This is my sanctuary.

I see the women of the world becoming stronger and stronger as we group together and bring out the unique qualities we have. I think women have more power than they know. We have more options than men. We can be masculine and feminine at the same time and society accepts it. We can be totally unisexual, wear anything we want - boxers, jeans, work boots, whatever - but it's not the same for men. They aren't allowed to dabble in different things like wearing skirts or women's underwear. The only thing they can have out in the open is their sexuality. Everything that is important - their emotions, their beauty, their true voices - is kept hidden inside. They start out as little boys, all cute

and sweet. Then society taints them. Boys need to be raised and taught to balance both masculine and feminine. To do what they *feel,* not what someone else *thinks.*

I'd like to see men who have a sense of balance, who can be sexual and have their emotions, who can get angry and work it out, who can say, "I'm angry and this is what's making me upset and I want to talk with you and see how you feel about it." Who can communicate and be okay about it. If men are sad, I'd like them to be able to say so, to tell others that they need their support. It hurts me that there aren't more men like Anthony, who can be positive and feel confident in their opinions, or unsure but willing to be unsure in the face of societal pressure. Men who can stand up and not be changed or influenced by the destructive messages they get. Men who can be strong, not use drugs, not swear or be derogatory about women or men or other races. Men who are stable, who will do positive things in their life. Men who don't use their strength to hurt women or others. Men who think before they speak.

When I imagine my future, I want my partnership with a man to be based on equal sharing, with lots of love and honesty, stability and security. I want it to be a relationship where both of us can take care of the kids. I want it to be free, where you can run around naked if you want to and be open. I want a home where whoever makes the mess cleans it up. As far as traditional roles for women go, I don't believe that women should stay home and not work. I want to be married and have a family, but I also want to work. I've never thought of myself as having one job or main task anyway. My mother always tells me, "Create your job." My dream is to teach and have enough time to love and care for my children. If I should marry an artist who couldn't financially support me, I wouldn't mind working. What's most important is the love we have for each other and sustaining that relationship.

What concerns me, though, is the future of my children's children. I'm worried about the Earth, their Earth, because I see so many people treating mother nature without respect. Picking at her, pulling at her, chopping trees, littering. What of the Earth will be

left for the future?

It's hard for me to understand racism, prejudice, discrimination, and why people do the things they do, because I feel that we are all the same. I'm scared and concerned about how poorly people treat each other. We don't see people for who they are. It worries me that we have so much poverty, so many people homeless. This is supposed to be the United States where we have so much, billions and billions of dollars, but there are people all over who don't have jobs or places to live. My mother always says, "Everyone should have a home." It's hard for me to understand why there's so much imbalance and disparity in the world. We have got to make ourselves and the Earth the priority. We have got to take more time to be with each other. We're all running around on these insane schedules, looking at our watches, saying, "Gotta go here, gotta go there." We need to relax and breathe and realize that we all inhabit the same place, we all share it, and in order to get anywhere, we're going to have to be together.

Daughters of the Moon, Sisters of the Sun

Linda Wolf talks with Byllye Avery

Byllye Avery is the founding president of the National Black Women's Health Project, an international self-help and health advocacy organization committed to improving the health of black women, particularly those living on low incomes.

Linda: What do you think most affects the health of black girls and women today?

Byllye: Most of the deeper health problems black girls and women have are stress-related. Rape, incest, domestic violence, volatile homes, guns, and gangs in school cause psychological problems which are compounded for those who struggle on lower income. I'm talking about black people, but you can see this across the board for all races and all classes. In general, people are so close to tears it's shocking. They're living with extraordinarily difficult realities. You can see it especially among low-income black teenage families. They're frustrated and feel hopeless. Many of them give up on parenting; it's just too hard. So stress is a very big issue. But I also see girls who simply don't care about their bodies. A lot of girls are overeating the wrong kinds of foods. This takes a big toll on their health.

Linda: What do you think is going to help black teenage girls' health the most?

Byllye: Psychologically, when they and their mothers are able to get their relationships together, things will be a lot better. And if their father is still on the scene, getting together with him as well. Another thing: when they're in the company of other black women and they feel comfortable, to be able to really talk about the hard things they go through, to sit and talk with each other about the realities of their lives. To ask each other, "What's really going on? What's been hard? What's happening in your life?" That's where the real growth is going to come from.

Linda: Tasha talks about how much hostility exists today in relationships between young black men and women. I've talked with a number of black teenage girls who defend rap music and say they don't mind the oppressive messages in some rap songs, calling women "hos" and "bitches."

Byllye: The little girls who say they love Snoop Doggy Dog and the little boys who are singing these lyrics are pretty ignorant. They simply don't understand what life's all about yet. They don't have the consciousness and sometimes, I think, facing reality is too difficult for them. Often, in the homes of these girls, there haven't been any strong women talking to them. They need to be around women who raise their consciousness about these things. They'll see it later on - once they see their mamas getting knocked clear across the damn room. That'll help them get it. We have to keep talking to them and remember that they do hear us. They might not do anything with it right then, but they do hear us. What worries me is all the girls who don't have anyone talking with them.

Linda: Do you see any positive results of the women's movement in the lives of the women you work with?

Byllye: Yes, the women's movement and feminism have been extremely important in helping to strengthen black women in general, but these movements have been mostly comprised of middle-income and educated women. The teenage girls and women who are experiencing the worst psychological violence are the ones living on lower income. Budget cuts and welfare reforms have removed many of the programs which are essential to helping lower income women. We need to help lower income women learn how to move on the inside, how to get things done, what options exist out there for them.

Linda: What do you mean?

Byllye: I'll tell you a simple example from my own life. I remember saying to one of my friends a long time ago, "Why is it a lot of white people don't have their teeth missing?" She said, "Well, because they get root canals." I'd never heard of a root canal. When I had problems with my teeth, the dentist never told me that there was another option, that they didn't have to be pulled out - they just pulled them out. Women who live on lower income need to know that they have options. I prefer to work with and speak to the realities and perspectives of these women because I believe when we work to help the folks who live on lower income, we lift up everybody.

Daughters of the Moon, Sisters of the Sun

Guadeloupe Maria Christo

My name is Guadeloupe, but I go by Maria. I'm Latin, nineteen years old, and I just got released from four years in jail.

I was eight and a half when my dad died. I didn't shed one tear even though he and I were really tight. I got real angry. We heard a big bang. He had been on top of the fourth floor of the house and was just laying there on the back deck. I remember him turning blue. Nobody knew CPR so they called an ambulance. The ambulance was late and they forgot to charge the respirators, so they had to use our electricity, which didn't work. If he would have made it into the hospital in time they say he would have lived. Some stranger snatched me up and took me away. I didn't know what was going on. I didn't realize for a long time. I didn't understand what 'dead' was. I made jokes about it because I didn't understand. My mom thought that I had no conscience.

I started getting drunk when I was about six years old. When I was twelve I left home, started smoking weed and getting affiliated with gangs. Then I got sexually assaulted. The guy had a knife and cut me up. I felt so much rage at that point that I turned into a different person. I started taking gang-banging and drugs real serious. I started curb-serving powder, building my clientele, and hooking up with a local Cryp gang. I tried to learn everything I could from the people who had the most status on the streets.

Just like in society, there's different classes of people on the streets. There's the lower class - like a prostitute, a smoker, an addict, a

junky. Then you get up into the gangsters - they get more respect and power. Then you get into the drug dealers. They make the money - they have what they want and they don't take any bullshit from anybody. Then you get into who supplies them with drugs and who supplies those who supply them with drugs, and where they go. And they go to the more elite clubs. It gets up to where it's actually into government. It's really crazy.

I was getting into all kinds of trouble - fights, conflicts, arrests, drug busts, shootings. I had so much money and dope on certain days, I would have to sleep right on top of it to protect it. Also, I had people after me for my life.

One night I was coming from one of my spots downtown and got pulled over and the cops searched me. I didn't have any dope, but they found my gun under the seat. They took me to the adult jail, fingerprinted me, took mug shots, booked me, and sent me to juvenile detention. They charged me with packing a pistol, a misdemeanor. I only had to do four days. Four days was nothing. But when you get locked up, you find out that the whole game is not genuine. Nobody's there for you anymore. But as soon as you get out, they come swarming.

When I got out, I went right back to the same old thing. I felt like I was untouchable, the hardest person out there. If I felt the slightest little emotion or sensation or feeling inside me, I'd cut it off, shove it down, and push it back. I thought I could do what I want, take what I want, say what I want. Everybody in my circle had my back.

I bought a '76 Thunderbird, gold, with a big stereo system, where I kept all my stuff. I was selling big bucks and hanging out with the hustlers. But for some reason I had a paranoid feeling. I started worrying about my mom and wanted to check on her. On the way, I stopped at one of my old spots and made a sale for $500. As I drove away, this unmarked car pulled me over. I was with some of my friends and they all had a lot of dope on them. I offered to hold it because I didn't care if they busted me. So I hid the dope in my bra.

I handed them a fake ID but they pulled me out of the car and said, "We know who you are. You have a federal warrant for delivering and transporting." They didn't care about my friends; they wanted me. A lady cop come over and searched me. She pulled my bra out but I was so nervous and sweating that the sacks just stuck to me. Then they tore the car apart. Tore the upholstery, the interior, popped the rims, popped the hood, and took the lid off the carburetor.

By that time there were three unmarked and about ten police cars, all with their lights on, blocking off the whole street. I was in the middle of the circle, just a little person in a big madness. Then they put me in a police car and took me way out to some old military building in the woods with sheets on the windows. I was scared because I knew when I got there they'd find all the drugs, so I took the sacks out of my bra and stuffed them up inside me. When we got to the armory, they put me in front of all these little microphones and grilled me. They took all the information I gave them and twisted it around to use as my confession. I never made a confession. I just made a statement. They didn't even tell me my rights.

I told them I was gonna be sick. They took me to the bathroom and were watching me, but I leaned over to where my shirt was hanging down so they couldn't see anything. I took my pants off, sat down, peed, and as I wiped I pulled the sacks of dope out all at once and flushed it down the toilet. I was like, "Oh God, if I stand up and that dope's in the toilet, that's possession of narcotics - another five years." I was really scared. I got up and looked down and it was gone.

I was charged with delivering and transporting of a controlled substance, three counts. My sentence was three to four years - the maximum sentence possible. I was sent to Echo Glen Juvenile Detention Center.

From the first day at Echo Glen I gave them an excuse to lock me down in my cell. I started fights and all kinds of stuff. I was out of control. I was so angry. I was trying to plan an escape for months. Then I don't know what happened. It started with this guy from the outside, Sherman Wilkins. He came and sat down on the floor in my cell and talked to me. He was the only one in that whole place that ever gave me any kind of respect - the only

ECHO GLEN
DJR

573 531

one who was really good to me. But I didn't really change until these ladies my mom sent, these Cuban ladies from a church in Seattle, came and talked to me. They just kept talking about how the devil had me by the strings and I was his puppet. They broke the Bible down and made it all relative to my life, my choices, my mind. They did something because I started reading the Bible and praying and getting back into my spirituality. I started changing and healing and letting go. And I cried for the first time. I cried for hours. I thought about all the times that I came so close to losing my life. I thought of all my friends that got killed, all my friends that killed themselves, and the ones in jail for life. I thought about what's really important. That's when I realized that even when I had been on top with all the money, I still wasn't happy. Sitting in that cell one day, I looked at myself and realized I wanted something better. I started to let people in and let myself feel. I got reality back.

After that I started taking advantage of every group there: Alcoholics Anonymous, Narcotics Anonymous, everything. Sometimes it was to get out of my cell, sometimes it was to learn something. Gradually people heard about me - people that had done prison time and got out and were real successful in the community. They would come see me, and a lot of seeds got planted in my head. I ended up graduating valedictorian of my class and when I got to the group home, I got a scholarship to intern as a mentor.

I learned you can't make anybody change. I know for a fact people have to hit bottom and learn for themselves. That's what life's about. And some people have to learn it the hard way. I wish I would have listened to people and taken their advice, but I had to learn the real hard way. Now, when I mentor other kids, I know I can only tell them what I know, what I think. I can sit and preach to them, but I don't have any hope in it being effective and sticking in their head. I can only plant seeds.

It's still hard for me. Some days I feel like I'm slipping, backsliding a little bit, even though I'll never be who I was, never go back. I'm still institutionalized, so to speak. I still feel the effects of the system. My goal is to live in the moment - take it day by day, keep a positive attitude, not backslide, and remember what's important and try and be happy. I want to make some kind of huge contribution to the world some day. I'm trying to be patient. It's funny - I longed for my freedom for so long, but then when you're actually out here, there's really no such thing as freedom because you're always confined either inside in your heart or in your mind or financially or something. So it's kind of like I'm still waiting for my freedom. A lot of times I feel rage, but not in the way that I used to. I feel restless, a kind of anxiety, and desperation. I don't know what it is. I feel like there's something that I'm supposed to be doing now that my life's not in danger, now that I'm in my right state of mind. I just can't figure out what it is. I know it's about giving back. I love being a role model for kids. They really responded to me and that felt so good.

I still have enemies on the streets, but when I see them I just turn the other cheek. I just say, "What's up?" and keep it moving. I'm respectful. I don't give 'em dirty looks, but I don't stop. They're still doing the same things. A lot of the people have disappeared or died or gone. The media - music and TV - they glorify violence, power, and gangs to all these young kids who are so vulnerable and easily influenced. These ignorant little 'gangstas,' they look like fools to me. They don't know what it's really about. It's a little game to them - gangs and drug trafficking. If they knew what it was really like and knew how the game was really played, they wouldn't want anything to do with it.

Guadeloupe Christo and Tasha Flournoy talk with Angela Davis

*P*rofessor Angela Y. Davis is known internationally for her ongoing work to combat all forms of oppression in the United States and abroad. Over the years she has been active as a student, teacher, writer, scholar, and organizer. In 1970 she was placed on the FBI's Ten Most Wanted List on false charges. She was the subject of an intense police search that drove her underground, put her in jail for six-

teen months, and culminated in one of the most famous trials in recent U.S. history. She was acquitted in 1972. Today she is an advocate of penal reform and a staunch opponent of racism in the criminal justice system.

Guadeloupe: What do you think is the biggest problem of the criminal justice system?

Angela: The criminal justice system is a kind of catchall for all the problems that exist in society - poverty, racism, and education. Rather than trying to address those problems in productive ways, the people who have the problems are just shut away.

Guadeloupe: Where do you see the system in ten years?

Angela: If it continues along the path that it is on right now, we will see a continued expansion of the prison system. When you consider that the welfare system has been practically abolished and that nothing has been developed as a solution, the fact that people in most states are required to work makes no sense unless jobs are available and unless child care is available and education is available. So if nothing changes, I think we will be moving toward what I would call an 'incarcerated society.'

Did you know that 1.5 million people are already in prison? If you can imagine 3, 4, 5 million people locked up, and many millions more on probation or parole or under the control of the justice system in one way or another, that is a very frightening prospect to me. If we don't do anything about it, the prison is going to serve as a model for so many other institutions. As a matter of fact, they're using the same kinds of models now in schools, so children who go to school often find a system that is not designed to educate them, but that is designed for purposes of discipline and security.

Guadeloupe: What do you think is the major problem with the juvenile system?

Angela: I think you can answer that question better than I. What do you think?

Guadeloupe: I think it's becoming more like the adult system. They are focusing more on punishment than rehabilitation and treatment. The security code and everything has become so strict, I just can't believe it. When I first got in, we had a lot of privileges. Now there's barely any. They don't give inmates a lot of contact with their families and they don't give them much support. The kids are real isolated when they need much more personal involvement, some one on one. One counselor has maybe forty kids on her caseload. Kids are just being kind of tossed away. What saved me was mentors and role models, people who came in from the outside to talk with me, people who could relate. I was fortunate. But there are a lot of people in the system that have no business working with youth or with any of the inmates, a lot of people who actually need some treatment themselves.

Angela: There's a very interesting book by a man named Jeffrey Reiman called *The Rich Get Richer And The Poor Get Prison*, which might be helpful for you to read. Personally, I think if more and more people would do the kind of mentoring that helped you, the barriers between the imprisoned population and the so-called free world would begin to drop. Because the whole system is a kind of mystery to most people, it is easy to create these kinds of stereotypes that have nothing to do with the actual human being. Of course there are some people who have done very violent things, but the majority of people haven't and they end up suffering. This ideological creation of the criminal prevents people from

understanding that there are a lot of criminals on the outside who damage people's lives and are responsible for people's deaths, but who are never ever called to be accountable. When you consider how many people die as a result of unsafe conditions on the job, but the executives of the corporations that are responsible for this are never treated as criminals and generally end up only paying a fine. Or when you consider the crimes against the environment…

Guadeloupe: I was wondering what your opinion was on why gangsterism and drug trafficking, violence, and those kinds of lifestyles are so glorified in today's society?

Angela: I think you may have a better answer. But I've noticed that education isn't represented as something that's exciting. When I was growing up in Birmingham, Alabama, the entire south was severely segregated. And I can remember that even though we went to substandard schools and got the cast-off, tattered books and had few resources and facilities, still there was a way in which the teachers made learning an exciting adventure, something we could look forward to. And I don't think there are many things in today's world that capture the imagination of young people, that can make them realize that the same kind of excitement that can be generated around gangs and gangsters can be generated around things that are productive and progressive. What do you think about it?

Guadeloupe: I think it has been glorified so much by the media, television, everything - music, videos, movies. And kids are so impressionable. They have been exposed to so much and they become desensitized. It's almost like sex and violence is the norm now. I think they're looking for something more, and they're really confused about the difference between power and respect.

Angela: I've been thinking about the way in which drugs are promoted in this society. There are the illegal drugs of course, but then there are all of the legal drugs. And consider the extent to which mind-altering drugs are prescribed to people and presented as the solution. Prozac is circulating all over. If you live in a society where drugs are so widespread and glorified, what can you expect? Violence has become the way in which people expect to entertain themselves. This whole war on crime, this notion that crime is on the rise and has been for the last decade or so, is not true. Studies have demonstrated that there haven't been significant increases in crime, but there have been significant increases in the representations of crime and violence in the media.

Young people today have to figure out how to create something that is collective and dramatic and exciting that will provide an alternative vision or that will provide a vision of the future. So many young people don't believe in the possibility of a future, of change. There's so much death and violence and destruction that many young people seem to give up. I think that the generation which finds itself in this quagmire is the generation that is also going to have to find a way out. Which means that young people like you have a lot of work to do.

Tasha: I am currently in an interracial relationship with someone I love very much. It's my belief that the more interracial relationships and biracial offspring there are, the less racism we will have - the less racism, the more quickly we can set about working on a better future for everyone.

Angela: Relationships are difficult regardless

of the racial composition. You always have to struggle to build any kind of successful and meaningful relationship. This is certainly a time in which interracial relationships are being legitimized, as well as a period in which people who emerge out of interracial relationships are thinking very deeply about what that means. We're realizing more and more that race is something socially constructed; it is not a biological essence. It was represented as a biological essence as the basis for a whole system of racism.

Tasha: I was wondering how you deal with everyday discriminations of all kinds, from skin color to sexuality.

Angela: I try to develop a sensibility that is anti-racist, anti-homophobic, that challenges gender discrimination, and that allows me to try to understand people who have physical and mental disabilities. It makes no sense to fight for institutional change if people do not change in their hearts. And that's a long, protracted struggle. It means we have to accept the fact that we are all influenced by these ideologies. Even though we may be the targets of those discriminations, we also internalize them.

Tasha: A lot of my black girlfriends feel disrespected, dissatisfied, and disassociated from black men. It's like the communication between black men and women is broken down. It's all about 'men are dogs' and 'women are bitches.' I don't know what we can do to improve the relationship.

Angela: One of the things that is helpful to me in thinking about how to challenge both racism and sexism is to think about these oppressions not so much as being embodied in people, but rather as being practices. You know that just because a person is white does not mean that person is racist. Oftentimes you see a white person who has developed much more advanced anti-racist practices than a black person, and the same thing can be true of women and men. Rather than seeing the conflicts and contradictions as gender wars, we can see them as struggles around the meaning of gender. Which means men can participate in those struggles in ways that place them in progressive positions, because there are men who are just as angry about the way that men are encouraged to think about women. It's time for men to organize in ways that women once did, to do the kind of education and serious consciousness raising among men that will begin to challenge some of these issues.

Tasha: Alice Walker's definition of womanism is "Womanist is to feminist as purple to lavender." Can you explain this?

Angela: I think that Alice was attempting to create a space for women of color to engage with the gender issue in ways that didn't necessarily link them with a tradition of feminism that excluded issues of racism. How do you talk about feminist traditions or womanist traditions in black history without suggesting that somehow feminism was created by middle-class white women and then we appropriated it for ourselves? There are long traditions among women of color, African American women, Latina women, Native American women, that indicate that we have been grappling with these questions of how to defend ourselves as women for a long time.

I've always been for crossing those racial boundaries, but it is sometimes necessary to politically distinguish ourselves from, say, a feminist who argues that the role of feminism is to open up the corporate boardrooms to women, because that will not make any changes at all. It will give women the opportunity to participate more equally in the processes of exploitation that result in the domination of poor women and men alike. I don't know whether it matters what one calls oneself. Sometimes I call myself a feminist, sometimes a womanist. I think the important thing is what one actually *does.*

Tasha: I have been struggling to know where I fit in as a woman of color. Can you give me any advice?

Angela: I think women of color fit in wherever they make a place for themselves and in accordance with our politics. I see 'women of color' as a kind of political project, a transformative political project, not as a description of some kind of biological, racial essence. It's really about changing the world. Therefore, I suggest you go where you think you can have an impact that's going to bring a more expansive consciousness to a large number of people, whether they're white or women of color. In a sense, we need to be everywhere.

Annie Huntley

This past year for me has been about healing myself spiritually, physically, emotionally, and letting myself feel the pain of my dad dying in April, my boyfriend Mike (the first person that I really loved) and I breaking up, then my friend Seth being in a car crash and in a coma.

Everything in my life was in place. I had my horse, my mom, my dad, and my brother. I had good grades and always had the money to do the stuff I wanted. Then, boom! I lost everything.

I didn't know how it was that someone could be given so much pain, so much loss. I lost it all. The things that are so important to me: connection with others, with Mike. I'm now realizing what it was I lost with my dad. I lost structure and I felt like I didn't have any anymore. I wondered, "Who or what else is gonna go?" There was so much fear. I was just waiting. It hurts so much to think about how I was. I had no perspective. I felt utterly alone, no matter how many people I had around me.

It was a great privilege to get the inheritance money from my dad dying and be able to spend the last six months over in Europe and Africa. Everybody says, "Did your parents help you out?" "Yeah kinda. My dad." I feel like he's helping me heal and I feel so much closer to him, and my mom, too. My friend Stephanie and I went to Europe in August. The biggest part of this trip was being away from everything that was going on and being with a friend that I knew would support me. We flew into Germany, stayed in Berlin, Paris, Spain, Portugal, Rome, Florence, Venice, and the Czech Republic.

Once, in Berlin, we were sitting at a bar and this guy from South Africa came over and started talking to me and he told me, "You are always alone. You're not your children. You're not your husband or your wife. You're always alone, even if you're married." My eyes filled with tears and that's when it really hit. Just a random guy from South Africa that comes and sits down, and I learned a very big, tough lesson. That was at the beginning of my trip and that's what the trip was about - being alone. It went from a very scary feeling of not wanting to be alone, into wanting to be alone. At one point I said, "Okay, I'm outta here. I gotta be by myself." So I decided to go, on my own, to Africa.

I realized that regardless of how I choose to perceive being alone, I will always be alone. I turned it into a positive thing. I don't need all these things that I had always searched for and thought I needed. Everything my Dad and Mike stood for - security from others, love and connection - when I began to find it in *myself,* that's when things started to change and that's when I was happy and empowered.

At one point Stephanie was in France and I was in Spain talking to her on the phone. She had seen this woman get the shit beat out of her by her boyfriend and no one did anything. She tried to run away from him but he grabbed her hair, kicked her feet out from underneath her, and just started pounding her. It hurt me so bad. I started crying and crying and I told myself, "If I ever see anything like that happen, I'm not gonna stand there and do nothing."

I went to Morocco and there was never a dull moment. Now Morocco's not a place where women's lib exists. If you're a woman, you're a slave. You're shit. You're a cook, a wife, a mother: anything that any *man* wants you to be. The men hang out on the streets at cafes, but the women aren't allowed in cafes. What really got me was that they're Muslim, but the women are not allowed in the mosques. I'm still trying to figure that one out.

I was walking down the street with a guy from France that I had met, and I saw this woman sitting with a little baby on her back and a three-year-old daughter and ten or twelve guys gathered around her. All these guys were yelling at her as I walked by. I thought, "Oh man, she's crying, she's got kids. Okay, wait a second. I've gotta do something." I went back and I tried to calm her kid down, and the kid freaked out. It got violent and these guys were just yelling at her. In my head I was thinking, "I don't know what's going on here. She could have stolen something from one of these guys." But ... that's fucked up, there are twelve guys against one woman with two kids. Then one guy came from the back of the crowd like he was gonna clobber her, and I stood in front of him and I pushed him away. I started yelling at them in French, "What are you doing?" I was so scared. My mind was jumbled. One of the guys said, "It's okay. It's okay." He showed me the ring. He said, "It's her husband." I said, "I don't care. Get outta here." So the guys went away and the husband grabbed the kids and ran across the street. The adrenaline was rushing through my body as I came to the realization that I would not allow myself to sit there and say nothing while something like that was going on. I felt good that I did something, but it brought up the hurt of seeing what these women are. Not *who* these women are, *what* these women are.

I got marriage proposals while I was there. There were two receptionists at the hotel I was staying at, and one night, one of the guys, in the middle of our conversation, held my hand and professed his undying love for me. I said, "Oh yeah, that's very nice." He said he had prayed to Allah for the last eight years to send him a woman, and that woman was me. I told him, "I'm sorry. It's not me." He wanted me to promise him that our hearts would always be together, even if we weren't physically together. I didn't want to hurt him. That's not in me. But at the same time I had to be true to myself. I couldn't lie to him. I could have so easily said, "Okay, our hearts will always be together." I told him about Mike and I said, "Allah wouldn't have sent you a woman that was in love with someone else back in the United States. It's not me. I'm not the woman. She's right behind me. She's coming through the door any minute." He was heartbroken. His eyes filled with tears and he left. I shut the door and turned around and started crying because I realized everything that he was saying to me was everything that I had said to Mike, and everything that I was saying to him

was everything Mike had said to me. That's what made me realize that Mike and I would never be together again. I cried in my pillow hysterically and then it was like, "I'm free." It was incredible.

The next night, his best friend, the other receptionist, came up and did the exact same thing. By that time I was mad. I said, "I don't pay money to stay here and get harassed by you guys." He told me that he loved me and asked me if I was a virgin. I laughed and said, "Wait a second, are you a virgin?" He said, "No ... I've been married." I started questioning him. "Let's say we get married. Can I go to cafes by myself?" He said, "By yourself? Would it be close to the house or will it be in town?" I said, "I'm gonna hop on a bus and take it to the other side of the country and go to a cafe if I want to." I asked, "About clothes, what am I gonna wear as your wife?" He started talking about traditional clothing (the women cover themselves from head to toe) and how it's changing, talking about how I'd need to dress. I said, "I'm gonna wear these jeans."

When you're married, you can't go any- where by yourself. I told him that I would be traveling for the rest of my life, alone, and he didn't even understand the concept. Wasn't in his reality. It wasn't a part of him. I had to honor him for that. What he knew was what he knew. At the same time, I had to honor myself for what I knew and what I was capable of. Still, with everything I told him, he didn't get it. He kept saying how I was the woman for him, so finally I told him that I was a lesbian,

"I only like women." He said, "What? How is it that you only love women?" I said, "Why do you only love women?" I started talking about the butt and the breasts and everything, and I said, "Okay, what do you think now? Do you think I'm still the one for you?" He asked how he could change me.

I went up to a town in the very north of the Sahara. I was walking around with a guide and he took me on a tour of the town. There were women doing the laundry in the irriga- tion canal, and it's a big thing to take pictures. I'd ask permission and go to take a picture, and the women would all cover their faces and hide themselves. That's a concept so foreign to me. It seemed that there was no pleasure in a woman's life. None. Then again, it's all relative. Maybe on the way back from doing the laundry they take a long route and go and sit in the field of flowers. I would enjoy that too. But I also enjoy traveling around the world.

I was in Marrakech, walking through the markets. The women don't work for money. They don't work in the shops, but there are some women who go through the markets with woven baskets, bracelets, or trinkets,

Daughters of the Moon, Sisters of the Sun

trying to sell them. That's when they've got their veils on because they don't want any of the men to recognize them. I felt such a connection to these women.

I think when most people see a woman completely veiled, speaking Arabic, trying to sell them stuff, there is a boundary; they don't understand them so they look the other way. But I saw through that. An incredible woman came up to me and tried to sell me a bracelet. I saw the person inside. I knew she could laugh and that she was just as I am, just as the next woman is, just as human, just as full, just as capable of living and feeling pain. She had everything that I had. We were trying to come together for two very different reasons. I wanted to make her laugh and talk (she spoke English). We just howled because she kept trying to sell me these things and make money. Money and connection! We did make that connection. We shared laughter.

For the last couple of years I've seen how everything has worked out in a sequential order for my benefit. I got a chance to get away from it all and evaluate what's been going on, and then I came back and there's so much more peace inside me. It's amazing to me how everything is working out. My mom always says, "You have to trust that the universe will take care of you."

What I have now is more security, more love, more connection than I ever had before. I did have it, but it was all outside of me. Now I know it's *in* me.

Bobbi Hervin

Most of my life I spent the entire summer with my mom, dad, and brother on a fishing boat in Alaska, scrubbing decks and cleaning salmon. We had a fishing business.

We'd get $60 for the season and they'd put the rest of the money away for us for college. When I was fifteen, I made a few grand and I spent it on a European vacation and a new vehicle. This year I want to save all the money.

Women just don't do the fishing thing. The guys think it's their job and that women can't be the captains of ships or the engineers or know all the technical stuff. It's hard work and it's very dangerous. Fishermen are uncomfortable having children and women around because much of what happens up there is sex, drinking, and dirty talk, so kids and women cramp their style. My mother was accepted because she was with my father, but having us kids on the boat was an incredible thing.

I think I was treated with a lot of respect, in part because they knew my father and also because I was pulling my own weight and doing a physically difficult job. One year I was on a boat my father owned. I was the cook, steered the boat, took my watches, and worked the hydraulics that tote the fish from one boat to the next, and I shoveled lots and lots of ice. When we were taking in the fish, I wore big slickers and rubber boots on deck because fish guts were everywhere. I don't mind getting dirty, but it can get kind of gross.

Now I also do the paperwork, writing the fish certificates after they sell the fish so they can be sure to get paid the right amount. Over time I've become famous for talking on the CB radio since that's another thing that women don't typically do. When I was up there two years ago, there was an all-women fishing crew and people always referred to them as dykes. The captain is a friend of our family and she is definitely not lesbian.

Journal entry

I have found a connection to the ocean that can never be broken. Since I was five years old, I have spent hours upon hours standing on the bow of our ship with the wind and the rain passing through my hair, watching the wake and churning water from the path of the ship's propeller for miles and miles. Today I know that if I am taken away from the Pacific Ocean forever, I will choke. As a child I did not pray to an almighty God above, but instead I spoke to the hills and the ocean, a power whose storms I thought truly governed the Earth.

Everything I've done and experienced has

made me stronger, including working on the boats. But the changes that happened after my dad's accident were really hard. When I was in sixth grade, my dad was in a car accident that left him blind. He couldn't fish anymore but he still ran the business and ran the boats. It was like that for a couple of years.

even though he was so sick, when he came home he tried to do as much as he always did, making plans for his boats and running the business.

Then about two years later, when I was sixteen, I began what I call my 'rite of passage,' taking over more of the business. I went up to Alaska and out on a boat. The second week we

Then my mom and my brother and I went to Mexico. When we got back from vacation, there was a message that my dad was in the hospital and it turned out that he had leukemia. Mom was devastated. He went into remission after a week of chemotherapy and

came into port and there was a message to call home. I said, "Oh no, something's up." I called home and found out that the leukemia had come back. When it comes back, there's little hope for recovery. I was in this town where I knew no one, all alone dealing with this. They didn't want me to come home, so I worked through the summer and I called him every week. A week after I came home, he died. I never really thought it would happen.

Journal entry

My life has been a series of awakenings and responsibilities taken while I was still quite young. I have handled the pain of the weight of a million stones, but I accepted them and carried them, knowing that everything happens as it's supposed to, as it always has and as it always will, for a reason.

Working on the boats has impacted my life and goals more than I ever would have imagined. Now I am ready to go to college and I always thought I'd study marine biology, but it's become so technical. I feel that things should be natural, so I have a hard time with technology. It scares me. Take salmon: there are so many that are raised in fish farms. They punch a hole in the fish and drop the eggs out and put them in a bucket, then squeeze the other salmon so the sperm comes shooting out. They mix it together and put it in a pot and pretty soon you have little salmon. Then they put them out in a stream and chemically program them so they will be able to come back to the same place. I just think it's wrong.

Massive fishing is absolutely disgusting too. I don't think it's right for the big trollers to be all over the world, going where they are not supposed to. I think it is a natural thing for us to take from the Earth to eat, and fish are already in the water. Not like cows that are raised for food and take all of our water resources. I'm becoming more interested in the social issues behind marine science and making the public policies, so I registered for a program called Environmental Health and Change.

Journal entry

If I should die tomorrow, everything will still be okay. My soul will simply continue swimming the sea for eternity. As for all the questions I've asked in my life, the Indigo Girls say, "There's more than one answer to the question." I agree. There are a million solutions to a problem and a million answers to a question. All that matters is that we ask the questions and merely search for and explore the answers.

These days I feel good about being a strong woman. I'm so used to being different and speaking out, but I am beginning to think about what I do more. For example: I shaved my armpits for prom. It was a tough choice and I feel naked now. I know hairy armpits bother people who have been raised with the belief that women are not supposed to have hair. They are genuinely disgusted and as much as I try to ignore that, I can't. If I am just being me and I notice that it's making someone else uncomfortable, then maybe I should be a little more careful. In most cases though, I do the classic "Whatever makes *me* feel good." Like deciding who to tell about my bisexuality. Some people you don't tell that sort of stuff to because they don't want to hear it. It's inside of me and it's something that I don't have to tell everyone.

I didn't have a traditional upbringing. I won't be studying a traditional program for women in college. And I don't always make traditional choices in my life. I'm learning how to be sensitive to other people and still be me. We don't always have to live in little boxes. The more I take risks with myself, in my life, I realize that the world's not so bad. I have to have a balance. I'm trying to find what makes *me* comfortable.

Journal entry

I believe in butterflies and quiet songs, in early sunrises and the stars at night. I believe in the moon during the day. I believe in long hair and decorating my skin. I believe in love. I believe that black and white are truly complex blends of a million colors. I believe in the ocean. Love is not just a term from the sixties; it's a power we give and receive every day. I feel that I love everything on this Earth and beyond. Love is a power that brings positive energy to the balance of good and evil in every person and element.

Dreams

Hold fast to dreams
for if dreams die
life is a broken winged bird
that cannot fly.

Hold fast to dreams
for when dreams go
life is a barren field
covered with snow.

— Langston Hughes

Tia Sharpe

My name is Tia. I'm eighteen years old and I attend, and play soccer for, the University of Portland. Sometimes I think I'm nuts.

My youth was centered around dreams. Dreams of being a good athlete, being beautiful, and being intelligent. The dreams would grow stronger as I studied the lives of my childhood idols and how they reached their goals. The overwhelming lesson was that achieving dreams meant hard work, so I adopted a strong work ethic and discipline. Looking back now I realize that there were two vital ingredients missing from my youthful pursuits: faith and joy. If I didn't reach my goal of being on the national team, then what? This is a question I never allowed myself to ask because I feared it might curse me to even contemplate what would happen if I failed. This left me with only one satisfactory option in life: success. I did not allow people to know just how lofty my dreams were because, if I didn't make it, I didn't want them to know I had failed. Living with this extreme self-imposed pressure kept me working hard, but over time I learned to view my soccer as a task rather than the game and artistic outlet that it is.

Joy and happiness were attached to achievements. When I made the Washington State team, I was happy. The Far West regional team added me to their roster when I was a sophomore in high school and, of course, I was thrilled. I was asked onto the Under-20 National Team as a junior, and playing for my country brought tears of joy to my eyes. But day-to-day life was drudgery because nothing could measure up to the immense high I felt when I was playing. I had to succeed at all costs because soccer had become my main source of joy.

My friends gave up on spending time with me because I was always playing soccer. I literally ran myself into the ground by my senior year of high school, when overuse caused a stress fracture in my left tibia. Dieting became a way of life and the more disciplined I was, the better I felt. Pictures from my sophomore year display the extent to which I tortured myself to achieve the figure I saw on all the elite players. I drank a vitamin drink for breakfast, the same for lunch with an apple and some crackers, and a potato and salad for dinner. Any nutritionist could have told me that was about the worst thing I could have done for my body during those developmental years.

Imagine living with a nagging voice that wakes up with you at dawn and falls asleep with you at night, reminding you of all the work you have to do - run, practice, lift weights. At the end of the day, as you climb into bed, you pull the covers over your head in order to hide from it, but it comes back to remind you that you didn't get around to lifting the weights today and if you ever want to make it big, you better get your act together for tomorrow. And the next day and the next. This is how I lived my high school years.

Over a year ago I broke my patella during a game. I had to wear a cast for three months and for the first time since I was a sophomore in high school, the nagging voice had nothing it could talk about. I felt free. The load was off my shoulders. Sleep came easier. Waking up no longer landed like a brick on my head. My logic told me I was supposed to dislike being injured, but my heart was at peace.

Unfortunately, I disregarded my heart as I had so often in the past, and found another area to apply pressure. I decided to attend summer school full time. I blew breath back into the nagging voice. I provided it with something new to get on my case about. The 'big man upstairs' tried all he could to get me to see my life from a new perspective, and he thought that breaking my knee cap would be enough, but he underestimated my stubbornness. I don't think the actual lesson came to me until the Lord finally pulled my ear to him and whispered directly inside.

There I was, sitting in bed at 10:30 p.m. on New Year's Eve, 1996. I was in Perth, Western Australia, visiting my parents. I could hear the music blasting from the bar down the street and people laughing as they walked by our flat, but I sat there in bed writing in my journal. I had pulled an article out of a magazine before I jumped on the plane in Portland. It was titled, "Reflect, don't resolve!" At the end of the article was a series of questions designed to help you look at your life on a deeper level. One question asked about my spirituality. I immediately wrote that I was spiritual, but I didn't have a certain religion in mind. Then I sat with my pen in hand and stared at what I had written. Was I really a spiritual person? Did I have faith in my life? No. I had become so blind to the simple pleasures of life that I could barely even see a big fat one when it sat directly in front of me.

I came home and called one of my good friends. She had been a Christian for about two years but had never pressed her views on me. As soon as she picked up the phone and we said our "hellos," I asked her for help. Asking for help is something a tough, driven, independent athlete isn't supposed to do. I asked her to help me develop a personal relationship with God. She saw that there was a seed of faith in me and from then on she has given me sprinkles of ideas when I needed them, but ultimately left the growing to me.

There is quite a bit of healing that needs to be done in my life as I listen closely to the conversations in my head. I pray that the nagging voice is heard and silenced. I say "heard" because to pretend it isn't there could be devastating. The joy is back in my life. I listen to the birds and see a new flower poking out of the muddy ground and truly let myself feel how special that moment is. When I am struggling through a hard practice, another voice inside me tells me to remember to enjoy every touch of the ball and trust that the outcome is inevitably in the hands of a much greater force.

Whatever your goal - athletics, beauty, intelligence, etc. - never let your dreams numb your perception of joy and happiness. Until a short time ago, I misinterpreted the poem by Langston Hughes. I thought it meant that if you ever give up on your dreams, your life would be as useless as a brown, wilted flower shoved in the pages of a dictionary next to the word 'almost.' Today I read the poem and feel it is reminding me never to lose sight of the child within me. We all remember this child. The one who soaks up the world with its big round eyes filled with curiosity and wonder, and who is content living each moment to its fullest.

Tia Sharpe talks with Michelle Akers

Michelle Akers is a world champion soccer player, Olympic gold medalist, and the leading goal scorer on the U.S. national women's soccer team.

Tia: When did sports become such a big part of your life?

Michelle: When I hit middle school, I started to notice my friends and other girls stop being so competitive with guys in coed games. I knew I could beat the guys, but I questioned whether the other kids would still like me. I wound up saying, "Screw it. I'm going to do what I want and if I can beat them, I'm going to beat them." That's when I decided I was going to beat whoever was in front of me.

Tia: Do you enjoy the emotional and psychological dimensions of competition?

Michelle: I love it. I love to be challenged, to be stretched, to do things that I haven't done before - things that scare me. I like to feel uncomfortable because I know it makes me grow, both as an athlete and a person. One of the greatest challenges of my life has been

being sick. What chronic fatigue syndrome has done is it allowed me to explore areas I couldn't or wouldn't have explored as an athlete. Being in athletics was the preview to me challenging myself as a person, rather than just physically.

Tia: How do you feel about the way women are pressured to be thin and to fit a certain stereotype of femininity?

Michelle: I think it's sad that a lot of coaches, elite athletes, magazines, media, and movies put so much emphasis on it. We had a nutritionist come in from Penn State to talk to us about how to eat right. She took a seven-day diet diary of each player and calculated the amount of calories we ate per day, broke that up into the percentages of carbohydrates, fat, and protein. The overwhelming thing she found was that every player on our team under-ate by at least 1500 calories a day, and that the fat intake was not enough. So these athletes were training for six to seven hours a day, eating low-fat and no-fat foods, when they should have been piling down the calories. We got the message loud and clear and made a special effort to get enough calories so we could be the best team in the world.

Tia: What kind of gender-related issues have you encountered in sports?

Michelle: Professionally, it's incredible to think the first women's soccer world championship wasn't until 1991 and the first women's soccer competition at the Olympics wasn't until 1996. It's because women weren't accepted as soccer players around the world; now we're big time. We have to fight for whatever we can. Often when we play overseas, people take videos or pictures of us just because we're women playing soccer. And believe it or not, some people yell or spit at us or make fun of us because they think women playing soccer degrades the sport. My reply to people like this is to tell them to come out and watch us. When they do, they love us. We have to be patient until people get over this kind of ignorance. We have to remember that every time we step on the field, we're selling women's soccer, whether it's on the national team level or a club team level. I must say that earning gold medals has quickly changed a lot of people's minds about the status of women's athletics.

Tia: Oftentimes female athletes don't fit the 'feminine' role models in the way they dress, act, play tough, etc. It's not that we're unfeminine; we're just being ourselves. How have you dealt with this in your life?

Michelle: When I was in high school, the normal standard of being feminine was long hair, make-up, a lot of style in your clothing, not necessarily dresses all the time, but you definitely didn't dress in the sweats and jeans which is our normal stuff today. I tried to do some of that, fleetingly, and said, "I hate this, I'm going to be who I am." I think my team epitomizes one type of woman: competitive, fierce, aggressive, and driven. They don't need make-up. They're not concerned about what their hair looks like during training. They love men, but having a boyfriend isn't everything. We need to encourage young girls to be who they are and to wear what they want and to express themselves in a way that makes them happy, and to get away from these stupid stereotypes.

Tia: What are your weaknesses and strengths relative to your sports?

Michelle: Both as a person and as a soccer player, my weaknesses are my strengths. I train hard and I prepare, but sometimes I train too hard and I prepare too hard and too much. I'm stubborn and determined enough to never quit, but sometimes I'm too stubborn and I don't know when to give in. It's a double-edged sword. I got myself sick because of that drive, because of my unwillingness to quit when my body wanted to. But that drive has also gotten me out of that illness.

Wind: Was it hard for you to accept that you couldn't perform on the level you were used to?

Michelle: It was devastating. My physical ability and strength, power, and endurance were my trademark. It took a long time for me to accept that I would have to play with limita-

tions; that I would have to live my life with limitations. I went through about a month asking myself, "Can I be happy knowing I have the tools to be the best player in the world, but can't be?" After a lot of thinking, I decided that this was an even bigger challenge than being the best player in the world. It means playing against all odds, going out there anyway.

It's the first time I've had to give up. It's the first time in my life I've had to understand and realize that I can't do something on my own terms and my own strength. It has taken me a long time to become physically healthy again, more stable and at peace with myself, and to have the strength and wisdom to know that I'm special anyway and that God will use me no matter how I am. Before, I would be very uncomfortable because I would have to be the one in control of everything. It's been an awesome journey these past five years. The Olympics were a miracle. No way in hell should I have been able to play. I was sick and dehydrated. After every game Steve, my trainer, would bring me in, lay me on the floor, and start taking off all my stuff. Meanwhile, my team would be walking around celebrating and I'd be crying on the floor. They'd go to the post-game and I'd go to the training room and get IVs. It was really hard.

Tia: A lot of people assume it's a male characteristic not to cry, to be able to handle pressure, and not get emotional. As athletes, we've been asked to take on these 'male characteristics' in order to succeed, but I see it more as a contribution to team.

Michelle: Is it really a male characteristic to be able to control one's emotions? Or just being able to know when it's appropriate and when it's not the time and place? To me, you put your team before your feelings; you can cry to your coach in private.

Tia: Linda and Wind were asking me how I feel about some of the male-oriented language used in women's sports - like 'man-on.' Does it bother you?

Michelle: My mom had to deal with the same kind of language issue as a firefighter. I remember the word battles she would have over being called a fireman. Because of her, I consciously say firefighter, but I wouldn't go out of my way to correct a guy who said, "So, you want to be a fireman?" I'd say, "Yeah, I want to fight fires." I feel like if I jump on him

about it, then he's going to react like, "Oh, you're one of *those* women." I feel like I can *show* him I am one of those women by who I am, rather than make this big deal about one word.

Tia: I agree. What bothers me, though, is the way the referees treat us compared to the way they treat the men's team. There are times when I want to go out and sit down with the refs and say, "Listen, you are disrespecting us and all other females by calling our game so much tighter, pretending that women can't get hurt, saying that we're not supposed to swear, giving yellow cards for things that you would never give to the guys." This is where I find sexism seep in.

Michelle: Yeah. In 1991 I went to Zurich for a conference about the future of soccer. During the conference I was asked by a referee about my thoughts on the refereeing of women's soccer around the world. My answer was more diplomatic than this, but I basically told him that I think it is atrocious. He listened to me and was receptive to my opinion and made an effort to comment to soccer's international governing body. I think refereeing is changing and we have to maintain a good attitude and educate people.

Linda: Are you independently wealthy now?

Michelle: No! Good question. I got an income on the national team in '95 and '96, basically a teacher's salary. I made money this year with Reebok, but not like the multimillion-dollar deals for some male athletes. Women soccer players - millionaires ? God, I'd love to see that!

Wind: What advice do you have for young people?

Michelle: My advice to young people is go for it. Don't hold back. Live the day like you're not gonna see tomorrow. Express how you feel. Take risks. Try new things. Look inside your self and be challenged. Live life to the fullest and don't be afraid of what other people will say or think. Don't let others squash your spirit. Be who you are and be proud of that and be happy with that.

The Other Side of Sports

Linda Wolf

Today it's rare if a school doesn't have a girls soccer or basketball or track team. From little girls to senior citizens, women are increasingly getting a chance to cultivate health, discipline, personal development, team spirit, and balance.

This is one of the rare domains where girls get positive reinforcement for what their bodies can *do,* not for what they look like. It's a place where social exclusion doesn't work, where team effort is everything, regardless of differences. This is exactly the environment we need to resolve the bigger issues we face in the world, and exactly what we're saying we want from guys. But this is only one side of the world of sports: the side which exalts the very best in human beings and human excellence. The other side of the story is not so pretty.

Traditionally, the world of sports has been dominated by men. At present, nearly 100 percent of the governing bodies - amateur and professional, national and international - the sports associations including the Olympic committees, the management and coaching staffs, the sports departments in all major media - television, newspapers, magazines - are dominated by men. There are women coming up the ranks to take positions previously held only by men, but we're a long way from equality. Laura Vescey, one of the few women sports columnists at a major metropolitan newspaper, told us recently that of the three thousand credentialed journalists covering the Super Bowl, maybe twenty are women.

When women do gain a foothold in this world, they are subtly attacked by the advertising that surrounds and supports sports on every level, driving both positive and negative stereotypes of men and women deeper into our collective psyches. For example, a recent magazine ad shows a photograph of a man's pelvis. All you see is the area from his waist to his upper thighs. Squeezed into the front pocket of his tight jeans is a Casio mini-television. The copy reads, "Get the entire USA Women's Hockey Team in your pants." In a magazine ad for Dare perfume, Lynn Hill uses impressive shoulder and arm muscles to hoist herself up a steep mountain. The caption reads, "Lynn Hill - world champion rock climber." In a second photo she lounges on

her side wearing bare-shouldered evening attire, makeup, long pearl earrings, moussed hairdo. Yet she still grips her coiled pink-and-black climbing rope as if she plans to use it during the evening's events. Caption: "Lynn Hill - Daring Woman." These aren't subtle messages; they're the ones we're accustomed to.

We're also accustomed to the masculine environment of the playing field. What do boys call boys who can't or don't do well in sports, or who cry and show emotions while they play? '*Girls.*' Or 'wimp' or 'sissy' or 'faggot' - all terms which imply someone weak, powerless, emasculated. Why is it that 'girl' is the worst thing a boy can be called?

Well-meaning athletes, coaches, and parents don't realize what they're doing when they yell at girl players, "Guard your man," or scream, "Man-on." This old way to use language subtly carves the sexist grooves deeper into our brains, making it that much harder to change what we accept as reality. But nothing cements it more firmly than the way sexism, homophobia, racism, and violence are tolerated in the manly world of sports.

According to Mariah Burton Nelson, author of the book *The Stronger Women Get,*

Daughters of the Moon, Sisters of the Sun

The More Men Love Football, battered women's shelters have documented that there are more reported cases of wife-beating on Super Bowl Sunday than on any other day of the year. Men talk about being pumped up from the game, pumped up from having all their buddies around, and getting angry when a wife or girlfriend either doesn't serve them food fast enough or makes what they consider a stupid or embarrassing comment while they are watching sports with other men.

Susan Brownmiller in her book *Against Our Will* writes, 'Against oneself, violence proves toughness. Against men, violence establishes a pecking order. Against women, violence serves as the ultimate control mechanism." Newspapers are full of headlines about male athletes being charged with sexual assault: twenty members of the Cincinnati Bengals football team; five Berkeley football players; five members of the St. John's University lacrosse team; five West Virginia University basketball players; five Kentucky State University football players; four Portland Trail Blazers ice hockey players; four Washington Capitals ice hockey players; four Duquesne University basketball players ... the list goes on and on. Why?

Of course, not all male athletes or fans are like this. More and more men are coaching their daughters and sons and taking them to see women's games, many parents are playing friendly coed games on family teams; and athletes are speaking out against the violence. There are more women in sports as managers, coaches, players, and owners than ever before - women who are paving the way for the next generation of girls who will advance and hopefully expect even more equity and opportunity and an end to the violence, misogyny, racism, and homophobia that must be countered. If the policy recommendations of the Amateur Athletic Foundation of Los Angeles have their intended result, televised sports news will provide more serious and respectful coverage of women's sports; announcers will adopt a standard usage of first and last names for male and female athletes of all races; female athletes will not be called, 'girls' (unless they are); and there will be less sexual objectification of nonathletic women during televised sports programs. And hopefully men will continue to wake up, stop using their brute force against people, and start using it to change the world.

Morgan Hohn

My name is Morgan. I'm seventeen. For a long time I thought I was dealt the bad card. I was never skinny; I developed breasts in fourth grade and got my period in sixth, and I've always had a big butt by magazine standards.

Daughters of the Moon, Sisters of the Sun

When I was in fifth grade, I'd cry and go into depressions for months. After about two years of careful and empathetic comforting, my mom basically got fed up and said, "Who the hell do you think you are? Nobody has a good life unless they make it good. We've all got pain. All you have to do to get rid of it is change your point of view and your expectations about yourself. Relax about your body. Look at your positive points." My dad was really important in helping me, too. He always praised doers, accomplishers. Through my parents, I realized that it wasn't so much how someone looked but what shined through them from inside that made them beautiful.

So I started incorporating what they said into my life. I started exercising and looking at my body for ways I could make it healthier, not just thinner. I still wanted to be thin, but sports showed me that I could use my body for something besides decoration. I started playing soccer, swimming, running track, doing water polo.

About this time, our family was showing signs of falling apart. My older brother, who was unhappy in high school, found a kind of family in the Christian church and wanted me to join him there. He became very zealous about it all and would scream at me over his beliefs. At first I used to fight with him. I would say, "Well, how come God is not a woman?" He'd kind of laugh at me and say "Because the Bible always says 'He'."

I always believed that you can't fight something unless you know about it, so I started going to church youth group. I went every week and the funny thing was, I liked it. But as the years got on, I realized that parts of the experience didn't feel true to me. I knew all the pat textbook answers like, "Who created the Earth?" "I know - God." "Who's God?" "I know - Jesus." But something inside me couldn't accept it all and sometimes I couldn't even say why. I was already looking for bits of wisdom in other places and experimenting with other things. I thought that to be a well-rounded person you had to try everything. So I stopped going.

I'm on a spiritual quest, but mine is to be at peace with life and myself. To walk down the street and see different-looking people, to talk to somebody, to argue, to be able to go to school and continue learning, to be in love, to be a woman - it's all a gift of life. I worry about what's going to happen in college or the fact that I wear a size larger in jeans now or could be better in art, but when I get quiet and recentered I think, "But I've got it made. I've got angels all around me. There's so much to life. Who needs to waste time unhappy?"

Before my senior year of high school, I was sent to the nongovernmental organization forum in China, held in conjunction with the fourth United Nations World Conference on Women. I had a hard time before I left because I wasn't sure what I had to offer there. I couldn't exactly say what girls in the United States needed, because all I could see was that girls here are so fortunate. What I learned in

Beijing is how on the outside it looks like we have everything, but on the inside, a lot of us feel like we don't even know what's missing. And in other places in the world, even if girls do know what's missing, they don't know what to do to change it.

Being in Beijing was incredible. All the color, the different faces and clothing, and the sounds of different languages. Right away I felt a renewed sense of purpose, especially after I met the official U.S. youth delegate for the United Nations, Janie Munoz, and she told me she wanted to set up a meeting with a few of us from the Youth Tent so that she could bring our message back to the U. N. official meeting. I was so excited. I ran up to one of the youth facilitators I really respected and told her. She looked at me and said, "If you think you can make a difference, I'm sorry you're here. The U.S. government plans and approves those speeches three months in advance." I felt like I'd been kicked in the stomach. Here I sacrificed so much to come and I felt that I didn't belong.

The next morning I ran into a friend who was feeling the same way. We were sitting around feeling depressed together when another woman came up who was part of a co-counseling program called 'No Limits for Women.' Her job at the conference was to run support groups. We spent the next hour talking about how we, the youth, can change things for the positive in the world. It was great, considering that each of us had this crap poured all over us that we couldn't make a difference, that we're not smart enough, that we'll sound stupid if we open our mouths. After about twenty minutes I realized that I wanted to start support groups for girls all over the world.

For the rest of the conference I facilitated a group every day. All together, including me, there were six of us: Annameika from Holland, Ericko from Japan, Kalyani from India, Bumi from Nigeria, and Navalene from the Netherlands Antilles. It had been raining all week, and one day when we met, a lot of people were crowded into the Youth Tent to stay dry. During a break in the rain, we took the last six remaining folding chairs and set them outside. What I most wanted to know was what it meant to be a woman. Not just an American woman, but a woman without cultural bonds. As we sat in that circle, my five friends and I,

with all the mud, in China, on the sidewalk, I was so happy to rediscover what I already deeply knew. That to be a woman takes whatever a girl or woman feels and thinks it takes. It is whatever she decides and chooses for herself.

Not only did we agree on what it takes to be a woman, but also on what helps us along, what helps us to find our voice on this journey. It is to have a safe place, a place outside of the norms and expectations of society, to be whatever you want to be. A safe place, a room, a house, an hour, time to sit and be heard, to hear others, to compare, to contrast, to find out, to filter through information and find where it fits with our selves, each in our own way. That was the most important understanding I brought back from Beijing.

Right now I'm experiencing what it means to really love someone and to be loved in return. My boyfriend, Charlie, and I call each other 'home.' It's not that he's half of me. We are complete people on our own. We don't need each other to exist. He is a friend. We trust each other, talk about everything, go places with each other's families. We have conflicts and arguments, but we listen and learn

from each other. There's nothing superficial about how we are together. Nothing is for show. We can be ourselves with each other. I don't have to suck in my stomach when I'm around him.

I don't know that Charlie will always love me or that I will always love him. Nothing's guaranteed. If we separated, I would still be a healthy person. I'd go on with life and he would be a wonderful memory. There's no pact or promise we can make except to be honest with each other and never to hold anything back. If we ever feel that we aren't happy together anymore, we'll separate. What makes him the most amazing friend I've ever had is the fact that we're able to connect on

every level, especially spiritually. We believe that we're walking through Heaven right now, that we really don't exist, that we're all one, and that we're all God.

Personally, I don't belong to any one party or religion. I'm not Democrat or Republican. I'm not Catholic or Presbyterian. Give me a point and I'll tell you my opinion. People argue with each other about who's right, but after a while it doesn't matter. Life is too short. Like my brother. I could argue with him about every little point that we disagree on. I could tell him I don't believe God is just male because he couldn't understand all humanity that way. He could show me every reference in the Bible to disprove me. But I'd rather have Thanksgiving dinner together and enjoy him because we're both human and from the same family. I am no longer seeking points of conflict or determined to make people see reality the way I do. If there's something I want to stand up for, something I strongly believe in, nothing will stop me from saying it, but I'm going to choose my battles, not fight in all of them.

I think I'm well-adjusted in a weird sort of way. Not in the socially prescribed way

Daughters of the Moon, Sisters of the Sun

because that would be like giving the pat answers in church. But like my mom. She doesn't fit the definition of the 'good mother.' She never does a dish, the house is always dirty, and she doesn't spend all her time cleaning and making everyone food. She spends her time creating and doing what she loves. And that's what makes her beautiful and well-adjusted. I simply do not want to fit someone else's standards and stereotypes. I want to remake them. As for the future, I dream that I'll travel someday. I want to have children but I don't need them to complete me. I don't need a lot of money either. I'll make my life beautiful with whatever I have. Above everything, I know that what's most important to my life is to love and be loved and to share with others what little bits of wisdom I've collected along the way.

A New Definition of Power

Linda Wolf

A new definition of power requires a complete shift in perception from 'power over' to 'power with.' Take any of the problems we have in this world - social, political, economical, environmental - and you'll see they all have to do with the way we use and abuse power, the way we dominate instead of partner up. For too long we have been run by the notion that the mark of a civilization is the 'strong-man rule.' Think of what we could do if we worked together.

In the 1960s, many of us stood up for civil rights and peace. Even when we participated in nonviolent forms of civil disobedience, we quickly learned what happens when you oppose the powers that be. Riot police come smashing in with their batons, rifles, dogs, mace, and fire hoses, scaring you into never wanting to speak out again. It's the same for people's revolutions in China, Africa, Guatemala, East Timor, Tibet. Politics is about power: who's got it, how it's defined, and how it's carried out. The people who have it don't want to lose it, and if you don't follow the status quo, you're an outcast in a dangerous position, a revolutionary criminal no matter how nonviolent you are.

Women are revolutionaries. We did not get the vote in 1920 by kindly asking men for it. Nor were we allowed to attend universities or become doctors or own property or hold rights over our own bodies just because we wanted to. We won't get equal pay for work of equal value if we don't have the courage to stand up together with our brothers and sisters and to demand our human rights. We won't stop the violence against us, or the persistent and increasing burden of poverty, or the brutish behavior of men during armed conflict, or the inequalities and inadequacies of health care, or the unequal sharing of power and decision-making, or the insufficient mechanism to promote women's advancement, or the lack of respect for and inadequate promotion and protection of our human rights, or the stereotyping of women, or the inequality in the media, or the inequalities in the management of natural resources and in the safeguarding of the environment, or the persistent discrimination against and violation of the rights of girls - unless we take up these issues one by one and do something about

them. These are the critical areas of concern adopted by the Fourth United Nations World Conference on Women, held in Beijing, China, in 1995. It's up to each and every one of us to make sure they are not ignored and forgotten.

Morgan Hohn talks with Bella Abzug

*F*ormer U.S. Congresswoman and former member of the U.S. House of Representatives Bella Abzug is cofounder and current president of the Women's Environment and Development Organization and a leading activist at the United Nations.

Morgan: Ms. Abzug, I would call you fearless for the kinds of things you've done over your lifetime. As a lawyer you defended people from McCarthyism and you worked with civil rights trials in Mississippi. As one of a few women elected to the United States Congress, you were a strong opponent against the war in Viet Nam and the first to call for President Richard Nixon's impeachment. Throughout your career you've consistently battled to

change the laws in favor of women and families. You've been called many harsh names for all this. So where are we today? What are the biggest issues left to do?

Bella: I don't think women are sufficiently involved in decision-making. I see no reason why we shouldn't share the political space fifty-fifty in Congress, in the state legislatures, in the local councils, and in the private sector itself. I think women have a different view, a transformational view. They see the potential of a world in peace, a world that's free from environmental degradation, a world that has human rights, equal rights, and economic justice. As you read various studies, you see that the gap between rich and poor keeps widening, which is a serious thing for civilization itself. I think women have to come into political and economic power and bring their view of a structurally transformed society with them.

Morgan: What do you think the next generation should do to carry this work forward?

Bella: We cannot have such divisions between rich and poor or people who would attack others by reason of race, religion, sexual orientation, or economic status. This cannot go on. We must change it. I believe that women, because they are not tied to the policies of the past - since they didn't let us participate in making them - can make the difference in changing the world viewpoint. In 1995, at the Fourth United Nations World Conference on Women, representatives of 189 countries came to an agreement on issues essential to women worldwide and created a document called the 'Platform for Action.' My organization took that document and adapted it to the problems of women in the United States. We call it the 'Contract with Women of the USA.' In it we project the women's agenda which governments and people have agreed to. It's up to us to see that it gets carried through.

Morgan: What kind of changes must there be to make it easier for men and women to participate equally economically and politically?

Bella: If women are going to have to work outside the home, as most women do, there have to be proper institutional changes which consider how to balance work and family. We're only beginning to deal with this in our country. There must be more meaningful maternity leave, paid time-off, better child care systems, and a greater understanding of the need for flexible hours and adjustments for families to be able to function in a way that their lifestyles require. Right now, the economy is being controlled by a few powerful forces. Some countries today have less power than some big multinational corporations. Our job is to say we cannot allow this to continue if we want to see society go forward. It is fundamentally a matter of control and power that we, as women, have to be leaders in changing.

I believe that this Earth can no longer function in the old ways, whether in the form of religious practices which oppress women or economic practices which eliminate social programs for women and children or in politics where the people who insist on remaining in power resist sharing power with women. I believe the transformational view that women have about life itself is the only way we can expect much change in this country or this world. The struggles women are conducting all over the world against laws, against religions, against practices, against customs which bind them to a patriarchal past, are very significant and very important - not only for women but for men - because we're all affected by what those who control power believe the status quo should be. We all have to change the vision. It's much harder for men, who have accepted certain practices and certain ways of life, to make the changes than it is for women, who have largely been outside of power. I believe that women are the change agents who are going to make the difference as we move into the third millennium, the year 2000. We want men and women to be there to help make the decisions that can improve everybody's life.

Daughters of the Moon, Sisters of the Sun

What the Women of the World Want

Morgan Hohn

DEDICATED TO MY BLOOD SISTER

You know what the women of the world really want?
It's to know that they're somebody's sister. They want to let loose their clenched jaws,
howl their cries of pain and frustration, and know that someone out there has listened
and accepted this great release, taken it in, nurtured it, held it as healthy and real,
and then released it back in as a new form - smoothed over, clean-breathing, and
whole - where it can no longer deflate or defile but become part of a strong realization
no longer locked within: the realization that she was and no longer is a slave
to someone, a slave to housework, to a frail body, to a fat body, to magazine ads,
to politics, to her brothers, to her husband, to her sons. A slave who has no say in her
household, no recognition for her hours of raising children, no acknowledgment for
sustaining the health of her family, no priority for her own health care, no teachers,
no education, no food at dinnertime, no sleep, no private space,
no choice in who she has sex with, and no voice.
But as long as this one woman, this one everywoman, owns her pain, owns her
screams, owns her doubts, she owns herself. The sister she longs for is the one who
will take in her sewage, her crap, her smoldering baggage. She is someone she knows
and doesn't know, recognizes and doesn't. She is the only one and the every one who
reaches out a smile, ear, hand, andhour, and knows what it means to be a slave.
She is a human being who has time to care about humanity. She is the only one and
the every one who can heal the world. She is the sister that each of us is asked to be.
She is the sister that we must be. She is the sister to the world.

FIVE

GENDERTALKS

Are Men Really From Mars and Women From Venus?

Wind Hughes

Men and women have long been thought of as sitting on opposite sides of the fence, like two different species staring at each other, trying to understand what their eyes and ears behold.

There's a lot of talk about how men are from Mars and women are from Venus and never the twain shall meet, but I don't believe it. And the more we view each other that way, the longer we perpetuate the idea that most of our differences come from inside us rather than from outside us. At times we seem so different it's hard to consider that some of these differences may not be biological. Instead, they might be learned - and what's learned can be unlearned.

The hardest part is trying to uncover exactly what biological and emotional differences really exist and how much, if at all, they affect our behavior and capabilities. After all, there are physical and chemical differences between members of the same gender too. In some cases, there may be bigger differences between those people of the same gender than between individuals of the opposite sex.

Psychologists - even feminist psychologists - are not in agreement about any of these questions, and researchers from different areas in psychology look at these questions from different perspectives. Physiological psychologists are looking for biological and chemical reasons to explain these differences and see them as arising from inside us. They are most likely to consider them unchangeable. Developmental and social psychologists look at the culture, society, and environment a person lives in to identify what a person is learning. If the roles, expectations, values, and status in the society are different for males and females, they will exhibit different learned behaviors. Evolutionary psychologists consider what they call 'adaptation problems.' We evolve according to what our environment requires for our survival. If our survival no longer requires a behavior, we might lose it, and if our environment changes to require new skills or behaviors for survival, we will develop those. It would follow, then, that if males and females require something different to survive, those skills will evolve to become a part of that gender.

With all that said, what do they find? In general most psychologists agree that, beginning at an early age, males exhibit more aggressive behaviors than females. There are also intellectual and cognitive differences, though they are mostly considered small: for example, women's higher verbal skills. A larger difference appears in 'spatial rotation,' which refers to the ability to track a three-dimensional moving object such as an arrow, an animal running, or a ball moving in the air. Males show a higher ability here. Evolutionary psychologists might say it's because our survival depended upon men's hunting skills, while social psychologists would consider that these skills are reinforced and valued for boys in our culture.

Psychologist Carol Gilligan proposes that there is a difference in moral development and that girls are more likely to develop a perspective based on caring and boys a perspective based on justice. Other research suggests that males are much more likely to touch a female than vice versa. Does this mean males are more demonstrative of their affections or is it, as some propose, that people of status and power are more apt to touch what they have power over and that people of less power or status are less apt to stop them? Research also indicates what the general population knows very well: that females and males have different communication styles. For example, males interrupt women five times more often than women interrupt them. My experience as a therapist would support this. But my experience has also shown me that communication patterns can be unlearned and new ones developed, to the point where men and women can acquire the same abilities over time.

Even though differences do appear, their causes and significance are still being debated. Some people believe that you can't even compare men and women in general because other factors, such as race, culture, and social class, outweigh the differences attributed to gender. Many feminists are concerned that this research could be used to oppress women and that any assertion of biological differences between the genders will be used to 'prove' women's inferiority.

The question of gender differences has been asked for a long time. I think at this point the only thing that is certain is that as many questions are being raised by these findings as are being answered. I know that I personally see a lot more similarities between the genders. Men aren't from Mars and women aren't from Venus. We're all from Earth, speaking the same language but different dialects. — Any translators?

GenderTalks

Wind Hughes and Linda Wolf

As the old story goes, many people achieve enlightenment in the cave but lose it when they return to the city. The same goes for many women who find their power and their voice only to lose them again when they enter relationships, especially relationships with men and the patriarchal culture.

As with any new experience or ability, we need ways to test our power, to temper its strength. This is one of the reasons we began to meet with the Boys Focus Group. We wanted to give the girls the opportunity to test their strengthened voices in dialogue, to help them build their confidence, and to practice not losing themselves in the process of relationship.

Another reason we organized the GenderTalks is that we must learn how to create cooperative, equitable relationships with all people, especially between the genders, based on mutual respect and mutual empowerment.

Many girls grow up hearing about the differences between men and women - different abilities, different chemistry, different biology - and the resulting 'inadequacies' and 'inabilities' of women. Equitable partnerships are almost impossible to create when one of the partners is perceived as more powerful and able.

In our GenderTalks we attempted to create an environment where the participants could move beyond the false concepts of who we think we are. We hoped to foster an openness to the discovery of how we can support each other in our differences and similarities. We wanted to provide an opportunity to hear each others' wants, feelings, and concerns and to attempt to bridge the gap between genders.

After a year of meeting in their own focus group, the young men were ready to meet with us. As you'll see in the following story, at first we approached each other with caution. That melted away as we truly listened to each other with open hearts and minds. We explored the differences between men and women and attempted to create understanding and cocreative partnerships.

Navigating the High Seas of Relationship
Christopher Love

*C*hristopher Love, facilitator of the Boys Focus Group and co-facilitator of the GenderTalks, is a registered counselor, certified clinical hypnotherapist, and certified neuro-linguistic program practitioner in private practice on Bainbridge Island, in Washington state. As cofounder of the Hidden Cove Institute of Relationship Studies, he offers workshops for corporations, adults, and youth.

The young women had been meeting for over a year when I was asked to facilitate the Boys Focus Group. From the beginning, I wanted to be a silent witness to the boys' process. I didn't want any of my 'stuff' to influence it. I intended to help them talk, to facilitate their awareness of deeper levels of feelings, and to provide a safe space for expression of those feelings. Our task was to prepare to talk with the young women in future GenderTalks. It wasn't always easy.

One day I mentioned to the guys how our attitudes about sex are conditioned by the media and the information we receive from teachers and parents. I mentioned that direct experience is our greatest teacher and emphasized the importance of sharing from the heart. One of the guys blurted out, "How about sharing from the hard-on?" Laughs

broke out and I realized I had just lost control of the group. "That was quick," I thought. For the rest of that session they cut loose in celebration like a gang of pirates as they discussed sex, taking on cartoon-character voices like Beavis and Butt-Head. This strange mixture of adolescent behavior, wrapped in a language of lust and cartoon voices, was reinforced and cheered on by the others.

As the sessions continued week to week, one recurrent issue emerged. Young men feel a tremendous amount of guilt which stems from several sources: knowledge that what most feminist women are saying about men is true; knowledge that women have not had equal rights and are not getting paid as much as men for the same job; and knowledge that many men are still treating women like subordinates and supporting the objectification of women's bodies. Another source of guilt and shame is men's violence toward women. While issues around emotional battering, rape, incest, and molestation cannot and should not be ignored, the knowledge of their existence leaves some young men feeling confused, guilty, and, at times, afraid of women, especially powerful women.

After a year of weekly meetings, we are invited to attend a GenderTalks session with the girls. In preparation I ask the guys to share their hopes and fears about the upcoming meeting. The expression is of collective FEAR. They are scared. They say they don't know what to expect. They are afraid that the women are in better touch with their feelings and that they will be intellectually massacred and emotionally battered. Some feel they will have to take "the women's crap for all the other men who have abused them and all women in general." I ask, "So what do we need from the women?" A young man quickly answers, "To be heard - I need girls to be patient and listen while I try to put my feelings into words." Another says, "It takes two to take responsibility for failure and good times. I need them to take responsibility too."

The day of the GenderTalks meeting arrives. From the beginning, the mood in the room is friendly but tentative. It isn't until the end of the day that the conversation moves to

a profound and new level. I ask the young women to go to one side of the room and the young men to go to the other. I hand out blindfolds to everyone and say, "With this blindfold on, it's easier to say what you might not normally say, so give yourself permission to go deeper than ever before into yourself. Our job is to speak and listen from the heart."

When the blindfolds are in place, Wind asks the young women, "What do we want from men?" Here are some of their responses:

"I want to be listened to and appreciated for who I am. I don't want to be looked down upon, I want to be respected."

"I want men to understand where women have come from, where we have been in the past, and where we are now in society's eyes. I think it will take a lot of synthesis and understanding of what has happened to move on in life in a way that is loving and respectful."

"I want men to stop letting things slide. When you know something isn't right, do something about it. It's not equality for women to have a balanced relationship with just women. Our reality is just as important as your reality, our way is just as important as yours."

"I would like there to be enough trust in a relationship, whether it is a friendship or an intimate relationship, that things can be talked about; so things big or small can be brought up and no one has to be embarrassed about it or feel awful about it."

"I would like men to enjoy themselves, enjoy life, enjoy their bodies, and enjoy my body too, in a healthy and respectful way."

"I would like men to ask us about *us.* When you don't know and you are confused, when you can't figure us out, I want you to be comfortable coming to us and getting to know us better."

"I would like men to not be unconscious about the way we make love to each other. Allow yourselves to get into whether we feel pleasure, or if we have been touched in the right way. I need to have more sensitivity from you. I would like you to be touching me in a way that feels good for me rather than touching me in a way that *you think* may feel good for me."

"I would like to ask men to stop stereotyping and let women have equal opportunity, pay, good jobs. Don't have us doing most of the work at home. I want you to really help us make a change for both of us."

Then I ask the young men, "What do we want from women?" Here's what they say:

"I would like to be able to walk down a city street and smile at or say 'Hi' to a woman, or be able to pick something up that she has dropped and hand it to her, without her thinking I'm doing it out of some bad intentions."

"I would like to be judged for more than just the image I project. Many of the women today voiced an interest in listening. I feel like I enjoy listening. I know trust has to be earned. If you haven't tried talking to us, it's not always bad. I need to be heard, too. Listen to me so you might see and judge what is under all that image that I sometimes portray."

"I need women to realize that there are guys out there that just don't fit the stereotype at all. The idea that you have to find the guy that sucks least, *sucks.* You have to look at us as individuals."

"When you are meeting or looking at someone just on the surface, the flaws have a tendency to dominate. It would be nice to look past the flaws and not just tell us what we are failing to do. Tell us what you have really enjoyed, what has made you happy. Sometimes we do stuff right and it goes unnoticed, so we stop."

"I would like to ask that women don't

look down on themselves for their image, either. Because everyone's beautiful, men and women."

"I want women to share about intimidation by men. Because I'm intimidated by men and by women. I need to be more open about it. I think everyone needs to be more open about people intimidating people."

"I would like to ask women to be patient as we grow and discover what it truly means to be a man."

"I would like to ask women to believe in us and to believe we are trying to do the right thing. If I'm doing something wrong, feel free to check me on it. I want an honest friend."

As we remove the blindfolds and sit in silence for a moment, we all just look at each other. Soon tissues are being passed out and both young men and women are wiping away tears. We all know we have experienced something very special: honest, heartfelt communi-

cation. For a few moments there is silence in the room, then people start commenting.

One of the young men speaks up first: "It's like we have been staring at each other all day; now, after the blindfold process, it's like a rebirth. I wonder if anything's really changed? Maybe most males have an image or a front or something, but most of us have what you women are looking for. Most males have it, but we also have a front. It's kind of like a little present. You have to open it."

"I liked what you said about how we should tell you guys what you're doing right. It is so true. Everyone needs to be told what they are doing right or they'll just ditch it, or they won't have respect for themselves. I don't think we do enough of that, no one does enough of that."

"We need to talk more. When we are together, we need to say, 'This feels good or that doesn't feel so good.' We need to share who we are," says another young woman.

Then a young man asks, "Do you guys get an overall theme from this whole thing? For me, I feel content. We're all just chilling

Daughters of the Moon, Sisters of the Sun

here, it's coed and it's cool. All the social issues are just out the window. I have this content, calming feeling."

"How often do we take the time to be together like this?" a young woman asks. "It needs to happen more often. It needs to happen every week." There is agreement around the room.

"Where do we go from here? Is there something we can do to help each other? We have to keep this unity. It's tight-knit groups like this that help, and when we're all really close, it's contagious and people respect that. We need to take what we have here and show others. We can model what we have created here today."

"Whatever we need to do to stay on the right track, we need to do! We could meet one-on-one or meet like this every few weeks. I feel I trust any of these guys to call them up and tell them I need to talk."

Then one of the young men says, "When we hear a guy say something sexist like 'Nice ass' or something, we should make a commitment to say that it is really not okay to hold an attitude about women like that." Another says, "I will!"

One of the young women adds, "I would like to say something to men when I hear them speak like that. It really bugs me. I'm not sure how to do that."

"Just don't rip him apart would be my advice. Give him a gentle word about his behavior. Respectfully address it," says one young man.

"I still think it's about listening. I noticed that a lot that was said before the blindfold was, 'You do this or you did that.' After the blindfold it was, 'Would you listen to me?' 'Would you listen to me' is a lot more appealing than 'You are not listening to me'," a young man boldly says.

A young women jumps in to say, "It's not about being right or wrong, otherwise you get

that hasn't been mapped out yet. At times in relationship this looks like trying to navigate a big sailing ship with no crew, in the middle of the huge open sea, towards a tiny island, at night, without any navigation or sailing experience. But we need to take the giant leap, take the risk. In the heart of the risk is the greatest reward: a life of equality that happens with the children, in the bank account, in the kitchen, in the bedroom, and in our hearts."

There is silence for a moment and then everyone breaks into laughter. Some make comments like, "We are doing it!" and "I love you!" A

wrapped up in the blaming. You just need to work on what works best for everyone, accommodating each other. We can effect change by just touching one person each. We are eighteen people here today. If we just touch eighteen more people, we then have thirty-six."

I share this thought, "We are on a path

Daughters of the Moon, Sisters of the Sun

mood of celebration ensues, a knowledge we have just made some kind of positive progress in the evolution of humanity.

One of the young women speaks through some tears and says, "I would like to be reminded about today. I want somebody, one of you guys, a year from now to come up to me and say something like, 'Do you remember what that was like that day?' Sometimes people start to lose it, you know? I really want to see it stay."

Epilogue

Young people often say that what keeps them from speaking honestly with teachers, parents, and counselors is a sense that they will be judged negatively. They find it difficult to establish trust with adults when this fear of judgment is present, especially when that person is in a position of power over some aspect of their lives.

When asked where they do share their feelings and concerns, they most often say they share with their peers or nowhere. We found the girls in our focus groups were hungry for someone to truly listen to them and eager for someone with experience to guide them - not to judge or evaluate them, but to listen, to offer information, and to candidly share their own experience and guidance.

Our success has largely been due to the fact that we provided what they asked for: no judgment, a willingness to hear it like it is, equity instead of superiority, and our honest experience and information rather than advice and directives. Another important factor was that all of the group members thought it was cool that their words and ideas were important enough to be a part of the project and this book. They felt respected and valued. Last and very important was the group's ability to call us on our stuff whenever they felt it was necessary, and they did so on more than one occasion.

Almost all of the older women who visited the focus group as mentors said, "If only I could have had an experience like this when I was young." We've been asked on many occasions to help others start groups like ours. Even though we have started many groups, we have never created a manual. But we can outline what has worked for us to create the kind of group that doesn't want to end.

We share this outline with you, not as a structure made of stone but as a guideline, a stepping stone towards the creation of groups where our lives as women can be shared and the gap between the generations bridged with love, respect, and the mutual excitement of a shared journey. The kind of relating this ingrains in us is what we believe will heal the world.

STRUCTURE

Size: Thirteen members is a great number because there are never too many or too few at any given meeting. Determine how many weeks the group will meet, with the option of continuing longer if the group desires. Once the membership is determined, we suggest you close the group to new members so trust can be established and a deep bond can be formed. We did open the group to new members three times, at the end of a cycle or as old members graduated or moved. It took time to reestablish trust, but each new member brought new direction and life to the group. It's a trade-off. Guests need to be approved before coming to the group.

Diversity: Try to have a cross-section of income, cultural background, and age.

Logistics: Meet weekly at a set time and at a private location. We met for one-and-a-half hours each time. We started on time and did not wait for stragglers or linger to socialize after the meeting. Responsibility to the group is essential. It is important to differentiate a focus group from a social group. We did not charge a fee for the group. If you do charge a fee, we suggest that free spaces be available so girls without means are able to attend. All girls under eighteen years of age had signed permission slips from their parents.

FACILITATORS

Choosing Facilitators: In our case, we served as mentors and maintained the flow and focus, but facilitators do not need to be adults. If they are, we suggest they be adults who are not in any position of power or authority in the participants' lives, as that might create a conflict of interest and compromise trust and safety. A focus group is not a therapy group. Again, in our situation, one of us is a therapist so we were able to process deeper emotional issues as they arose. If any issues arise that are beyond the facilitator's ability to process, we suggest you refer the girl or girls involved for professional help.

Topics and Direction: This is a cocreative process: the facilitators and the group together determine what topics will be discussed. We occasionally brought in reading material, films, and guest speakers to provide the group with information on topics of their interest. We presented our intentions to the group and if they approved, we arranged the event. The girls knew their attendance at these special sessions was important.

Due to time constraints, not everyone can process an issue at every meeting, so we began each session with a quick check-in with all of the members, asking if anyone had a burning need to share that day. When a member was speaking, it was 'her turn' and the rest of the group was to be quiet and listen, letting the speaker know that what she was saying was important to us all. In the beginning we used talking stones or sticks to identify the person who had the floor.

The most important thing is that each meeting be meaningful, processing issues deeply whether they are centered around pain or joy.

Mother/Daughter Meeting: After one year the girls felt ready to meet in a focus group format with their mothers. As facilitators, we prepared some questions and exercises for the meeting to encourage communication and sharing. We, and the girls, found it to be a moving, enriching experience, bringing the mothers and daughters closer.

GROUND RULES

1. It is fundamental that each member of the group understand that *everything* that happens or is said during a session is kept *inside* the group. An important part of this rule is that no one can bring up, at a future time, *anything* anyone says in the group without asking for permission to bring it up from the person who said it. This not only cements trust, but it also underscores the understanding that people are in process; that simply in the act of saying something and being heard, psychologically and emotionally, it is probable we have already moved on. We are constantly growing people; we are not static.

2. All issues and ideas are to be considered important. Nothing is considered an inappropriate topic.

3. We agreed not to talk negatively about each other outside of the group and to remind each other if we forgot.

4. Don't come to the group on drugs or alco-

hol. When members did, we left it up to the other members to decide how to handle it.

Conflict Resolution

We emphasized that conflict was a natural part of life and a challenge to look within ourselves and to embrace change. When conflict arose between members, it was handled immediately, with each girl in the conflict having a chance to express herself. Each member in conflict would listen to the other from the heart, and would repeat to the speaker what she heard her say, as many times as was needed till the speaker felt she was heard correctly and completely. Often just knowing they were truly listened to was enough.

The other members of the group often encircled the members in process, sending energy of support and love to them, and listened as witnesses, giving feedback if desired. We also reinforced the idea that it is okay to agree to disagree, as long as we respect each other in the process.

Flexibility

Staying on track was important, but we saw the group as an organic process, sometimes veering away from our intended focus. When a natural detour to a related issue arose, we allowed this as it often led to a deeper connection. We were careful not to follow superficial associations and would redirect the process back to the original path.

Closure

We end every focus group, GenderTalks, and workshop with an ancient ritual closing. On our final day together it was an emotional experience to hold hands in the circle as we always did, staring deeply into each other's eyes, knowing it was the last time we would say these words together:

By the earth that is our body,
And the air that is our breath.
By the bright fire of our magnificent spirits,
And the water of our living wombs.
This circle is open,
But never ever broken.
Merry meet, merry part,
And merry meet again!

Bibliography

Adler, Margo. *Drawing Down the Moon*. Boston: Beacon Press, 1979

Angelou, Maya. *Gather Together in My Name*. New York: Bantam, 1992

Angelou, Maya. *I Know Why the Caged Bird Sings*. New York: Random House, 1970

Brooks, Geraldine. *Nine Parts of Desire: the Hidden World of Islamic Women*. New York: Doubleday, 1977

Brown, Lyn Mikel and Gilligan, Carol. *Meeting at the Crossroads: Women's Psychology and Girls' Development*. New York: Ballantine Books, 1992

Budapest, Zsuzsanna. *The Grandmother of Time*. New York: Harper & Row, 1989

Chicago, Judy. *Through the Flower: My Struggle as a Woman Artist*. New York: Doubleday, 1975

Daly, Mary. *Gynecology: The Metaethics of Radical Feminism*. Boston: Beacon Press, 1978

Davis, Angela. *Women, Race and Class*. New York: Vintage, 1983

de Beauvoir, Simone. *The Second Sex*. New York: Modern Library, 1968 (original work published in French in 1949)

Duerk, Judith. *Circle of Stones: Woman's Journey to Herself*. San Diego: LuraMedia, 1990

Edmonds, Vicky. *Used to The Dark*. Seattle: e) all of the above, 1991

Eisler, Riane. *The Chalice and the Blade: Our History, Our Future*. San Francisco: Harper & Row, 1987

Eisler, Riane. *Sacred Pleasure: Sex, Myth and the Politics of the Body*. San Francisco: Harper, 1995

Faludi, Susan. *Backlash: The Undeclared War Against American Women.* New York: Doubleday, 1991

Findlen, Barbara, Ed. *Listen Up: Voices From the Next Feminist Generation.* Seattle: Seal Press, 1995

Friedan, Betty. *The Feminine Mystique.* London: Penguin Books, 1982

Garrison, Omar. *Tantra: The Yoga of Sex.* New York: The Julian Press, 1964

Gilligan, Carol. *In a Different Voice.* Cambridge: Harvard University Press, 1982

Gimbutas, Marija. *The Civilization of the Goddess.* San Francisco: Harper, 1991

Glendinning, Chellis. *My Name is Chellis & I'm Recovering From Western Civilization.* Boston: Shambhala, 1994

Greer, Germaine. *The Change: Women, Aging and the Menopause.* New York: Fawcett Columbine, 1991

Griffin, Susan. *Woman and Nature.* New York: Harper & Row, 1978

Haich, Elizabeth. *Initiation.* Garberville: Seed Center, 1965

Heilbrun, Carolyn. *Writing A Woman's Life.* New York: Balantine, 1988

hooks, bell. *Ain't I A Woman: Black Women and Feminism.* Boston: South End Press, 1981

Hurston, Zora Neale. *Their Eyes Were Watching God.* Urbana and Chicago: University of Illinois Press, 1978

Iglehart, Hallie Austin. *Womanspirit: A Guide to Women's Wisdom.* San Francisco: Harper & Row, 1983

Kilbourne, Jean. *Killing Us Softly: Romance and Rebellion in Advertising.* New York: Henry Holt & Co., 1998

Lacarriere, Jacques. *The Gnostics*. San Francisco: City Lights Books, 1989

Lerner, Harriet Goldhor. *The Dance of Anger*. New York: Harper & Row, 1985

Levine, Stephen and Ondrea. *Embracing The Beloved*. New York: Anchor Press, 1995

Mankiller, Wilma. *Mankiller: A Chief and Her People*. New York: St. Martin's Press, 1993

Martz, Sandra. *When I am an Old Woman I Shall Wear Purple*. California: Papier-Mache Press, 1987

Millet, Kate. *Sexual Politics*. New York: Doubleday, 1970

Morrison, Toni. *The Bluest Eye*. New York: Washington Square Press, 1970

Nobel, Kathleen. *The Sound of a Silver Horn: Reclaiming the Heroism in Contemporary Women's Lives*. New York: Fawcett Columbine, 1994

Noble, Vicki. *Motherpeace: A Way to the Goddess Through Myth, Art and Tarot*. San Francisco: Harper & Row, 1983

Paglia, Camille. *Sexual Personae*. New York: Vintage Books, 1991

Pipher, Mary. *Reviving Ophelia: Saving the Selves of Teenage Girls*. New York: Grosset/Putnam, 1994

Plant, Judith. *Healing the Wounds: The Promise of Ecofeminism*. Gabriola Island, BC: New Society Publishers, 1989

Rich, Adrienne. *Of Woman Born*. New York: Norton, 1976

Rountree, Cathleen. *Coming into our Fullness: On Women Turning Forty*. California: Crossing Press, 1991

Rowbotham, Sheila. *Woman's Consciousness, Man's World*. Harmondsworth: Viking Penguin, 1983

Shepherd, Linda Jean. *Lifting the Veil: The Feminine Face of Science.* Boston: Shambhala, 1993

Starhawk. *Dreaming the Dark: Magic, Sex and Politics.* Boston: Beacon Press, 1982

Stone, Merlon. *When God was a Woman.* San Diego: Harvest/HBJ, 1976

Weinstein, Marion. *Positive Magic.* Washington: Phoenix Publishing Inc., 1967

Wilshire, Donna. *Virgin, Mother, Crone.* Rochester: Inner Traditions, 1994

Walker, Alice. *The Temple of My Familiar.* San Diego: Harcourt Brace Jovanovich, 1989

Walker, Barbara G. *The Woman's Encyclopedia of Myths and Secrets.* San Francisco: Harper & Row, 1983

Walker, Rebecca, Ed. *To be Real: Telling the Truth and Changing the Face of Feminism.* New York: Anchor Books, 1995

Wolf, Naomi. *The Beauty Myth: How Images of Beauty are Used Against Women.* New York: Doubleday, 1991

Wollstonecraft, Mary. *A Vindication of the Rights of Woman.* Harmondsworth: Viking Penguin, 1975 (first published in 1792)

Woman of Power: A Magazine of Feminism, Spirituality and Politics. Cambrige, Mass.

Woodman, Marion. *Leaving My Father's House: A Journey to Conscious Femininity.* Boston: Shambhala, 1992

Woolf, Virginia. *A Room of One's Own.* San Diego: Harvest/HBJ, 1989

Zweig, Connie. *To Be a Woman: The Birth of Conscious Feminism.* Los Angeles: Jeremy P. Tarcher Inc., 1990

VIDEOS

Kilbourne, Jean. *Still Killing Us Softly: Advertising's Image of Women.* Cambridge Documentary Films, Inc.

Kilbourne, Jean. *Slim Hopes: Advertising & the Obsession with Thinness.* Media Education Foundation, Northampton, MA 01060

Pettigrew, Margaret. *Goddess Remembered.* Distributed by: direct cinema ltd. Inc., 1990

Marshall, Heather; Bassmajian, Silva and Pettigrew, Margaret. *Full Circle.* Distributed by: direct cinema ltd., Inc. 1993

Armstrong, Mary and Pettigrew, Margaret. *The Burning Times.* Distributed by: direct cinema ltd., Inc. 1993

WORLD WIDE WEB RESOURCES

Thanks to Jill Lippitt at ElectraPages for the following information. The ElectraPages are a searchable directory of over 9000 women's groups, including over 1000 World Wide Web links covering a comprehensive range of feminist issues and interests.

The Daughters/Sisters Project - http://www.daughters-sisters.org

American Association of University Women - http://www.aauw.org

Blue Jean Magazine - http://www.bluejeanmag.com/BJ/welcome.html/

Children of Lesbians & Gays Everywhere (COLAGE) - http://www.colage.org/

Club Girl Tech - http://www.girltech.com/

Cultural Environment Movement - http://ccwf.cc.utexas.edu/~cmbg/cem/

The Cybergrrl Webstation - http://www.cybergrrl.com

The ElectraPages Directory of Feminist Organizations - http://electrapages.com

Expect the Best from a Girl, and That's What You'll Get - http://www.academic.org/

Feminist Activist Resources on the Net - http://www.igc.apc.org/women/feminist.html

Feminist Majority Foundation Directory - http://www.feminist.org/gateway/master.html

Girls Inc. - http://www.girlsinc.org

Hues Magazine - http://www.hues.net/

Ms Foundation for Women Homepage - http://www.ms.foundation.org

National Organization of Women (NOW) - http://www.now.org

National Political Congress of Black Women - http//www.natpolcongblackwomen.com/

National Women's History Project - http://www.nwhp.org

New Moon Magazine - http://www.newmoon.org/

Teen Health Web Site - http://chebucto.ns.ca/Health/TeenHealth/index.html//

Teen Voices - http://teenvoices.com

UNICEF's Voices of Youth: The Girl Child - http://www.unicef.org/voy/meeting/gir/girhome.html

Women As Allies - http://www.Women-As-Allies.org/

Women Leaders Online - http://wlo.org

Women's Environment & Development Organization (WEDO) - http://www.wedo.org

Women's International News Gathering Service (WINGS) - http://www.wings.org

Daughters of the Moon, Sisters of the Sun

Photograph Credits

All of the photographs in this book are by Linda Wolf except for the following which we acknowledge with grateful thanks:

Cover photograph, by Gay Marshall;

page 26: Starhawk, courtesy of Deborah Jones;

page 31: illustration, "Enthroned" - Goddess of the Field, Pazardzik, Bulgaria, 4500 B.C., by Kristen Tonti;

pages 40, 134: courtesy of Wind Hughes;

pages 57, 59, 207: courtesy of Airyka Rockefeller;

page 105, 109: Indigo Girls, courtesy of Sony Records — photographers, Mary Ellen Mark and Michael Halsbrand;

page 127: Wind and Kimberley, courtesy of Wayne Fields;

page 132: Kimberley Hoffman, courtesy of Jim Mannino;

page 143: Wilma Mankiller, courtesy of James Schnepf;

page 148: Janet McCloud, courtesy of Jim Bancrof;

page 162: Guadeloupe Maria Christo, courtesy of the Washington State Juvenile Justice System;

page 182: Tia Sharpe, courtesy of University of Portland — photographer, Joanie Komura;

page 199: Bella Abzug, courtesy of Timothy Greenfield-Sanders;

page 228: authors, courtesy of Gay Marshall.

Linda Wolf (left) is a professional photographer and photojournalist. As cofounder of the Daughters/Sisters Project, she facilitates focus groups, workshops, and training for youth and adults. She is an organic gardener and ecofeminist, practises yoga and meditation, and aspiring musician, and lives with her husband, Tom Smeeth, and daughters, Genevieve and Heather, on Bainbridge Island with their two cats, three box turtles, scores of wild birds, and an assortment of visiting friends.

K. Wind Hughes (right) is an Individual, Marriage, and Family Therapist and Massage Therapist in private practice, and cofounder of the Daughters/Sisters Project. She travels, presenting a wide range of workshops and trainings. As a teenage parent, enthralled in the culture of the sixties, she found her youth a time of exciting and challenging self-exploration. Wind lives on Bainbridge Island with her partner, Christopher, and enjoys time with their grown children, her cats, guitar, garden, and rollerblading.